The *Wisdom* House

*You don't always have
to learn the hard way*

Rob Parsons

HODDER

First published in Great Britain in 2014 by Hodder & Stoughton
An Hachette UK company

This paperback version first published in 2015

2

Copyright © Rob Parsons, 2014

The right of Rob Parsons to be identified as the Author
of the Work has been asserted by him in accordance with
the Copyright, Designs and Patents Act 1988.

A CIP catalogue record for this title is available from the British Library

ISBN 978 1 444 74567 2
eBook ISBN 978 1 444 74568 9

Typeset in Garamond MT by Hewer Text UK Ltd, Edinburgh
Printed and bound in the UK by Clays Ltd, St Ives plc

Hodder & Stoughton policy is to use papers that are natural,
renewable and recyclable products and made from wood grown
in sustainable forests. The logging and manufacturing processes
are expected to conform to the environmental regulations
of the country of origin.

Hodder & Stoughton Ltd
338 Euston Road
London NW1 3BH

www.hodder.co.uk

*To my grandchildren — Harry, Lily, Evie, Jackson, Freddie,
and any others who may come along in the future!*

And in memory of my dear friend, Bob Marrable.

What they said about *The Wisdom House*

'I would love to put this book into the hands of every young person at the start of their working life.'
— Liz Jackson MBE, Managing Director, Great Guns Marketing, Inspire Business Awards Business Woman of the Year 2008

'I am almost eighty years old, but I believe there are fresh lessons of life in this incredible book. Don't miss them!'
— Dr R T Kendall, author of *Totally Forgiving Ourselves*

'Full of warmth, humour and insight — a joy to read.'
— Katharine Hill, author of *Rules of Engagement*

'*The Wisdom House* made me laugh, cry and everything in-between. Parsons has a rare gift — he is a true storyteller.'
— John Archer, winner of The Magic Circle Stage Magician of the Year, and the first person to fool Penn and Teller

'*The Wisdom House* is a treasure trove! It is a must-read for anyone, young or old. I wish I'd read it myself 20 years ago.'
— Sarah Abell, author and columnist for *Psychologies* magazine.

What they said about Rob Parsons

'Parsons is unlike any other business gurus ... he identifies an emerging social class – the new poor.'

— Des Dearlove, *The Times*

'The man who reinvented fatherhood.'

— Linda Lee Potter, *The Daily Mail*

'Rob Parsons has an uncanny ability for asking some of life's most challenging questions in an unobtrusive way.'

— Jill Garrett, former Managing Director,
The Gallup Organisation UK

Contents

Acknowledgements

AFTER TWENTY BOOKS, I want to put on record my incredible debt to Sheron Rice. Sheron is a brilliant editor and loyal friend, and has influenced every one of my books enormously. When I finish a manuscript and show it to her I feel as if I am waiting outside the head-mistress's study door to see what she is going to say. So from the bottom of my heart, thank you, Sheron, *again*. I wouldn't want to write books without your help.

Once again my publisher, Hodder, has been brilliant, and particularly Ian Metcalfe. Thank you to the whole team there. Thanks also to Michael Bates, Samantha Callan, Antony Elliott, Paul Francis, Bob Gorzynski, Kate Hancock, Jon Mason, the team at Care for the Family, and my agent Eddie Bell of the Bell Lomax Moreton Agency.

And of course, thanks and special love to my wife Dianne for all her input, support and . . . patience.

I

Welcome to the world!

IT WAS ALMOST midnight when my wife Dianne and I got the news – our new grandchild had just been born. We couldn't wait to see the latest addition to the family and almost dashed off to the hospital there and then, but good sense (and a pretty straight talk from one of our kids) kicked in, and we resigned ourselves to waiting until the following day.

I was shaving at about 7 a.m. the next morning when my phone pinged. It was an email with a photograph of the brand-new baby. I don't know why, but suddenly I felt compelled to write this child a letter.

Here it is:

Good morning, and welcome to your first dawn on this planet!

I gather it was a rough night. I'm glad that all went well eventually, but I do appreciate that after nine long months in that warm nest it might have been a little disconcerting to realise your mother had decided it was time for you to leave. I'm sure that as you now lie in her arms, you understand it wasn't personal – as nice as the scan picture was, she wanted to see a little more of you.

And I'm sure you know that you had a little difficulty exiting that nest. Those strangers coming at you with what looked like pliers were just trying to help. They were your friends – although it is worth remembering that if anybody ever tries to do that again they probably *aren't*, and it would be best to get out of their way.

Try to enjoy these first few days on earth – they are special in so many ways. First, everybody will want to know your name. It will seem to be one of the most important things in the whole world to them. But people are fickle, and in the years to come you might find that they do not treat it with quite so much respect. Some of them will change it or shorten it, just because they like it more that way – or worse, they will forget it completely. And another thing about your name: as you get older, you will discover that the phrase 'your name' means more than just the combination of letters that let people tag you. It comes to stand for the kind of person you *are* – to symbolise not just your identity, but your *character*. The world you have just entered is full of people who will want to take that good name from you, but don't let them. Guard it with all your heart.

And there's another reason to make the most of this time. Right now, everybody will say you are 'beautiful'. I'm afraid this wholesale admiration wears off pretty fast. Soon, some people will judge you by how you look, and some may even enjoy finding a few flaws. Don't let them get to you. And, above all, don't try to please them. They will rob you of the truth that you are special. (By the way, if your mother ever enters you for a beautiful baby competition, pack your milk, bottles and rattle, and leave home straight away. Playing that game when you're forty is hard enough, let alone when you're only a few months old!)

Oh, and a little word about your weight. I understand that you were seven pounds and three *ounces*. Enjoy that *ounces* thing, because when you leave the hospital, the people in the world out there only count in pounds.

In the next few days there will be lots of people wanting to see you. To be honest, some of them will be pretty scary – they'll make strange sounds at you, and pull funny faces. But the good part is that for this short time you will be the centre of attention, and that feels nice – enjoy it. The truth is that life is not always like this, and in the years ahead there may be times when it seems that nobody will even cross a room to speak to you – let alone cross a city.

Most of us, from the day we are born, try to find ways to make people want to cross that room to us. We quickly discover that if we are attractive, successful and – best of all in their eyes – important, they will practically knock the wine waiter over in their attempt to reach us. And so we spend our lives striving, accumulating and botoxing, all in the hope that we'll get people's attention. But that kind of life is so tiring – and, frankly, when most of them do get across that room to us, we find they are so fickle it was hardly worth our effort to get them there. Why, even as we are speaking to them, they are glancing around the room to see if there are any better prospects.

At those times, try to remember something very important. It is this: there is someone who will never forget your name and will always think that you are beautiful, no matter how many marks, scars or bruises the world you have just entered leaves you with. Your mum and dad could not love you more. Even now, when you are not yet one day old, either of them would gladly lay down their life for you. But the good news I have for you is this: even their love is not as great as the love that planned you, formed you, and now welcomes you into his world.

And so on this, the very first day of your life, let me set you on a treasure hunt: it is to seek out and find those and, perhaps especially, One, who will not look first at your appearance, achievements and status (impressive as those are), but who will love you *anyway*.

But enough of all that for now. We've got so much to do – dens to build, ants to watch, places to hide, ice creams to guzzle – and you've got naughty cousins who can't wait to push you around the park so fast you'll be hanging onto the sides of your buggy for dear life.

Good morning, our brand-new grandchild. It's time to play!

When I had finished my short missive and started shaving, I realised that I felt good about this letter. Here was I, a grandfather, doing what grandfathers are supposed to do – attempting to save this little one from having to do what most of us generally have to do: learning the hard way.

But pretty soon the good feeling went. I was assailed

by a barrage of imaginary friends all yelling at me, 'Who do you think you are, you old buffer? The baby is not yet twelve hours old and here you are making the poor thing sit in class.'

'And anyway,' one of the killjoys added, 'people *have* to learn the hard way. No pain, no gain. You can't put an old head on young shoulders. The school of hard knocks is the best education.' This doom merchant seemed to have an endless stock of these proverbs all ready to knock the wind out of the sails of anybody even thinking of passing on a little wisdom to the young.

I sighed and put my razor down. As I did, I caught a glimpse of my face in the mirror. I couldn't help comparing it to that of the new baby. In some ways our faces are similar. I am convinced that the baby's eyes are just like mine – at least, they would be if they were open. What is for sure is that our DNA is practically the same. If not for me, this new person would not be on this planet. And both our faces are a bit battered, bruised and lined – although, I must acknowledge, in different ways. The marks on the baby's face are from where forceps were used, and those will fade and go; the lines are folds of extra skin that would have filled out if this little one had been born on time, two weeks later, and soon they will go. The marks on my face, however, are so old that I can't remember how they got there – except for the dent that sits one centimetre above my right eye. (I was ten, and so was Richard Harries, who'd somehow got hold of an air pistol. He'd fired it at a wall and the pellet ricocheted off the cement and onto my head. I had a headache, but I didn't go blind. That centimetre's gap saved me and Richard Harries from a lot of trouble.) And what about all my wrinkles? Again, I have no idea where they came from. Over the years they crept onto my face like camouflaged soldiers. Some of them stayed . . . and those that did took their camouflage off.

No matter how I try to dress it up, it is an old face that I am looking at. But suddenly, as I gaze into the mirror, I am seized with a mission. I am going to banish from my mind the Job's comforters who say you can't pass on any wisdom to the young.

In my study are two chairs. One of them is mine – the one to the left of the fireplace is the chair I always sit in. And the other? Oh, that one has been occupied by so many different people – young and old, rich and poor, humble and arrogant, those full of hope and others sinking with despair. And, of course, the simple truth is that someone who has been all of those things – and more – has sat in *my* chair.

What conversations those chairs have heard down the years! As I stood in the bathroom on that Monday morning I thought how I would love to have the chance to sit and talk in my study not only with my newest grandchild, but with all my grandchildren when they are grown. Maybe these talks would be when they are about to begin their first job, buy their first house, get married or perhaps start a family. But I also imagined tackling more difficult subjects – perhaps talking with them long into the night, when their hearts were broken or friends had betrayed them. Maybe I could help them piece back together a dream somebody had trodden all over.

But I am at an age when I cannot be sure I will have those precious opportunities. There are too many years on the clock for me to be certain that I will be able to pass on some hope, encouragement and, once in a while, even a little advice. And then I remembered a story that my mother used to tell me when I was a child. It was about a village in a land far away where every elderly person would write down a life lesson to pass on to future generations. Each one was carefully written on parchment, rolled up and placed in a hut in the centre of the village. Once in a while, the elders would gather people together in the hut, unroll the parchments and read out loud the lessons that had been forged in the lives of those who had gone before. The villagers called that hut 'The Wisdom House'.

And so, with the shaving foam still wet on my face, I made my decision: I would create a 'wisdom house' for my grandchildren. I would gather together lessons from those in the second half of their life – including some of my own. I liked the idea of the village elders reading the lessons out loud, and so I decided I would imagine speaking face to face with my grandchildren. They are only babies and toddlers now – Harry (4), Lily (3), Evie (2), Jackson (9 months) and Freddie (7 months), but in my mind's eye, I see them coming into my study one at a time and sinking into the old leather chair – the one to the right of the fireplace – not as children but as the adults they will become.

And you, reader, are welcome to eavesdrop as I meet with my imaginary guests.

Welcome to the Wisdom House. Come on in.

2

Life's not fair

I T's GOOD TO see you! Take a seat. No, not that one – the one to the right of the fireplace. There are so many things we will talk about over the coming months, and there certainly won't be any order to them – these days I can't even find my glasses, let alone plan a systematic lecture programme! But however many or few lessons there turn out to be, I'll make sure I leave a copy of them behind – just in case, on a rainy winter's night in twenty, thirty, even fifty years' time, you feel like taking a read. After all, what have you got to lose? Most lives are filled with some happiness and some pain. If you are wise it is sometimes possible to get more of the first and a little less of the second. And I have written these to help you do that – not only in your own lives, but in the lives that you will touch.

So, sink deep into that armchair, kick off your shoes, and let's start.

Just yesterday, I heard one of you say to your mother, 'It's not fair, Mum!' I think your complaint was to do with not being able to stay up a little later. I wouldn't dare adjudicate on which one of you was right, but you will find as you get older that 'it's not fair' is often true of life.

This is such a hard principle to come to terms with. Most people understand the concept of fairness well. We know that without rules, a game isn't worth playing, so we like it when the referee spots somebody breaking those rules. We may be glad when an exam cheat gets found out because we know how unfair they are being to those doing the exam the hard way. But, of course, fairness is not an issue that only impacts us on the sports ground or in school. It is something that affects us in the deepest areas of our lives. Perhaps the most difficult theological question in the world is 'Why does God allow suffering?' Actually, although it's not often articulated, most people's question goes deeper even than that: 'Why do good people suffer?'

Because good people do suffer. Bad things happen to them. And when they do, the word on our lips is 'Why?' It's a good question, but you may never get an answer.

Of course, some people *try* to give answers. They say

things like 'Testing times make us stronger' or 'God is trying to teach you a lesson'. This is often because they find it hard to cope with this issue – to accept that things like pain and even death happen to good people. Later on, I want to write a letter that will touch on what I believe about life after this one, because that offers at least the possibility of some sorting out of the mess we find here. But for now, I want to tell you something that will help you if you go through bad times – or, if you've experienced them already, something that will help you deal with the memory of them.

This is an area where there is a real possibility of sounding trite, for no matter how great or small our pain, it is always all-consuming to us. Slick and easy answers do not diminish our grief – they multiply it. So let me allow you to listen for a moment not to me, but to a man who I believe will have suffered at least as much as anything you might have gone through already or may face in the future. See whether or not you think there is wisdom in Victor Frankl's counsel.

Frankl was a Jewish psychiatrist who experienced life in several of the death camps during the Holocaust. He spent some time at Auschwitz (a place I have visited twice). He was a good man, who spent his life trying to help other people. When the US Army eventually liberated Dachau, the camp he was then in, he had lost his wife, his family and his health, and he had seen more pain and suffering than any human being could be expected to bear.

When people asked him how he coped – how he went on not just living, but helping other inmates survive their own private hells – he said this: 'Everything can be taken from a man but one thing: the last of the human freedoms – to choose one's attitude in any given set of circumstances, to choose one's own way.'*

When the bad times come, we can be forgiven for becoming bitter, for seeking revenge, for ceasing to believe that there is a God who loves us. That is understandable. But Frankl says there is another way. We can *choose* a different response. We can choose not to condemn ourselves to a prison of a thousand 'what ifs?' We can choose faith over cynicism. We can choose to affirm that though it is broken and battered, this is still a beautiful world, with endless possibilities for redemption and hope.

Yes, life is definitely not always fair, and if you are going through painful or dark times that you never expected, I wouldn't be surprised if you said to me, 'Pops, you just don't understand.' Perhaps you'd be right. But I

* Viktor E. Frankl, *Man's Search for Meaning: An Introduction to Logotherapy*, 3rd ed. (Beacon Press, 1992).

also believe that what Frankl said is true. Life may have taken things from you that you never thought you would lose, but one thing remains which it cannot take . . .

. . . your choice as to how you will live tomorrow.

3

Living a life true to yourself

A LITTLE WHILE AGO, an Australian palliative nurse called Bronnie Ware began to blog about her experiences as she nursed people in the last weeks and months of their lives. These patients often shared their deepest feelings with her, and Bronnie said that time and time again they mentioned the same regrets.

She wrote a book about it called *The Top Five Regrets of the Dying.** I haven't spent as much time with the dying as Bronnie, but I can tell you that I have heard these same regrets aired by people – and not just by those who are near death, but by those who, in their later years, perceive

* Bronnie Ware, *The Top Five Regrets of the Dying* (Hay House, 2012).

that they have lived life in a way which has brought them little satisfaction.

The first one she mentions is: 'I wish I'd had the courage to live a life true to myself, not the life others expected of me.'

At the moment, there's a television series being broadcast called *Who Do You Think You Are?* It takes celebrities on a tour that delves into their ancestry and helps them discover their roots. If you've never looked into your family tree, you should try it sometime. Just this month, I found your great-great-grandmother listed in the 1911 census. She was registered as a 'widow'; only a few months earlier your great-great-grandfather was killed while working in a quarry just outside Cardiff. Her son, Clifford, aged ten, was listed in the census as well. Just five years later, that young man lied about his age at an army recruitment office, and months after that he was being gassed in the trenches in France. I also found your great-grandmother's name on the list; she was called Mabel, and she was just one year old.

The search to find our place on the family tree is interesting, but it's nothing like as fascinating as asking 'Who am I?' in a deeper sense. Of course, some people will laugh at that, saying that the answer is on your birth certificate, and there's no point in delving any further. But those who whisper that question to themselves know why they do so: it is because they have spent so much time trying to be like somebody else – perhaps to become the person others want them to be – that, along the way, they have lost their own identity.

Some of us have spent our lives trying to please other people: our parents, our teachers, our lovers, our friends. We have dressed in a way that we hope they will like, or we have taken subjects at school that they wanted us to study. We have tried hard to be witty, sexy, academic or sporty because we desperately wanted to be part of the group. Perhaps we have even taken a particular career path just to please somebody else.

I wonder if karaoke will still be around when you read this letter. In case you miss out on that little pleasure, let me enlighten you. Karaoke is quite a hit at parties. It's made up of two Japanese words, one meaning 'empty' and the other 'orchestra', and it allows people to sing along to well-known songs that other people have made famous. There's always a backing track, and you read the words from an autocue. If you really get into it as an art form, you practise the movements of the people you are imitating, and even dress like them.

But karaoke has at its heart a dreadful dilemma: the better you get at it, the more you look and sound like somebody else. Now, in itself, that's not a problem unless the day comes when you want to sing your *own* song.

Logically, there shouldn't be any issue with your doing this, but the second you open your mouth to sing you realise that you have no words or moves of your own. Pretty soon, the audience is yelling for you to switch on the same old backing track and climb into the well-worn costume again. And in that moment you discover that you have spent so much of your life trying to be somebody else that both you and the world have missed the person you *are*.

If karaoke was only played at parties it wouldn't be such a problem. But it's not. It is rolled out in schools, colleges, offices and homes. Some of us spend our whole lives trying to be somebody else. Shakespeare understood the inner torment of a life led like this and put into the mouth of a father some words of wisdom as his son leaves home:

> *This above all: to thine own self be true,*
> *And it must follow, as the night the day,*
> *Thou canst not then be false to any man.*[*]

The experiences we have, and the personality, gifts and talents that we possess, may not be what we would have chosen. (There's an old joke about a man complaining

---

[*] William Shakespeare, *The Tragedy of Hamlet, Prince of Denmark*, Act 1, scene 3.

about his looks and saying, 'When they were giving out ears, I thought they said "beers" and asked for two large ones. When it came to noses, I thought they said "roses" and asked for a big red one. And when they said chins, I thought they said "gins" and asked for a double.') But for better or worse, what we have is *us*. And, anyway, when we decide to work with what we've got, there are sometimes surprises, and what we thought were handicaps turn out to be rather different.

When Michael was a child, it didn't seem that he had a lot going for him. He had Attention Deficit Hyperactivity Disorder (ADHD) and had huge hands and feet which his classmates made fun of. He endured years of ridicule for those size 14s! But one day he climbed into a swimming pool. If you want to see somebody really cut through water, they are going to need many different attributes, but huge feet and hands is a great start. Michael discovered that the things that were holding him back when he tried to be like others were his greatest strength when he decided to be himself. What made him a source of ridicule on land made him a world-beater in his perfect environment: water. His surname is Phelps. He won eighteen Olympic gold medals, set a swathe of new world record times, and has a strong claim to be the greatest Olympian *ever*.

It isn't just seeming physical disadvantages that can

turn into a strength, but life experiences too – even ones that others would naturally run from.

Some years ago, a friend of mine attended a lecture in Oxford on stem cell research given by a world-famous geneticist. During the question time, the scientist was asked whether, in the future, it would be possible to clone Beethoven. His answer was a brilliant 'yes' and 'no'. 'Yes' if you could extract the DNA from the bones in his coffin – then you could create a human being who would be an identical twin of Beethoven. 'Yes' you could probably teach the 'twin' to play the piano to a reasonably high level. But 'no' because Beethoven's father, who was also his music tutor, was a violent alcoholic. The young Beethoven was very close to his mother, who died when he was a teenager, and he became responsible for raising his two brothers as his father lapsed deeper into alcoholism. He lost his first and only true love, he lived in poverty, weighed down with debts, he suffered from manic-depression and, like his father, turned to alcohol. Then, just as Beethoven began to have some interest in his compositions, he began to lose his hearing.

The culmination of all these experiences – the feelings of rage, love, despair, passion – was poured into his most famous pounding six symphonies (Numbers Three to Eight), which are what we now revere as 'classic' Beethoven. More accomplished musicians may now play or conduct his works, but they can never capture his greatness because that quality was born out of his expression of his own life experience, *of being true to himself.*

But being true to ourselves is not easy. So often, the reason we fail in it is because we want to present only the best aspects of our life and experience to the outside world, and hide the things that cause us pain. But like it or not, those experiences and our apparent weaknesses are part of who we are today.

So why do we so often overvalue others and persistently undervalue ourselves? Henri J. M. Nouwen put it this way:

> As long as you remain blind to your own truth, you keep putting yourself down and referring to everyone else as better, holier, and more loved than you are. You look up to everyone in whom you see goodness, beauty and love, because you do not see any of these qualities within yourself. As a result, you begin leaning on others without realising that you have everything you need to stand on your own two feet.*

* Henri J. M. Nouwen, *The Inner Voice of Love* (Darton, Longman & Todd, 1997).

In the film *Chariots of Fire*, Olympic runner Eric Liddell says, 'I believe God made me for a purpose, but he also made me fast. And when I run, I feel God's pleasure.' The truth is, we can't run the race on any track except our own.

I do know that this stuff is a lot easier to write about than to put into practice. But sometimes we must just find the courage to switch off the karaoke machine and announce to the audience: 'This is me.'

And then, for good or ill, give it everything we've got.

4

Wide-awake dreams

D O YOU DREAM? I'm sure you do. Somebody once told me that there are three common nightmares that many people have regularly: being naked in a public place, falling off a cliff (apparently if you hit the bottom in the dream you die in real life, but to date nobody has been able to confirm that), and being just a few weeks away from a major examination without having done any revision. I get that last one at least once a year (unfortunately for me, it is not so much a dream as a memory!).

Sigmund Freud described dreams as heavily disguised forms of infantile wish-fulfilment, expressed as hallucinatory experiences during the course of sleep. Freud may well have been the founding father of psychoanalysis, but is this sufficient to describe the power of a dream?

Another man had a different view of dreams, and it's his definition that I want you to consider today. Lawrence of Arabia, as he came to be known, grew up in Oxford, the 'city of dreaming spires'. Lawrence had a dream of an Arabia for the Arabs, free from the imperialism of the Turks, British, Italians and French. His was not a dream that was experienced during the course of sleep, but a vision worked out in the harsh sands of the Arabian Desert. In the introduction to his classic work, *Seven Pillars of Wisdom*,* he writes:

> All men dream: but not equally. Those who dream
> by night in the dusty recesses of their minds wake
> in the day to find that it was vanity: but the dreamers
> of the day are dangerous men, for they may act their
> dreams with open eyes, to make it possible. This I
> did.

Don't you find those last three words compelling? 'This I did.' In those three words is the determination not just to dream, but (even allowing for the possibility of failure) to give everything to seeing those dreams fulfilled. And it is a determination to have those dreams fulfilled not just for ourselves, but for the greater good. Dreams are

* T. E. Lawrence, *Seven Pillars of Wisdom* (1922).

not meant to be self-serving or vain hopes, but a powerful vision of where we want to be – both individually and collectively.

In his book *Soul Tsunami*,* Leonard Sweet writes:

> Institutions, friendships, marriages, corporations fall apart 'at their dreams'. You say: No, the metaphor is 'at their seams'. I say: No, the metaphor is 'at their dreams' because their dreams are their seams. Dreams constitute the new grand narratives, which are in short supply in post-modern culture. Dreams are the visions and vibrations.

On 28 August 1963, Martin Luther King stood on the steps of the Lincoln Memorial in Washington DC and looked out on a crowd of two hundred and fifty thousand. The majority of those people had been subject to beatings, shootings and systematic prejudice because of the colour of their skin. They had brought their grievances to the capital and looked to their leader to inspire them with hope. Dr King began reading from his handwritten speech, but for some reason the great orator was not managing to connect fully with the vast and expectant crowd.

---

* Leonard Sweet, *Soul Tsunami: Sink or Swim in New Millennium Culture* (Zondervan, 2001).

Just as he was nearing the end, the famous singer Mahalia Jackson shouted out, 'Tell them about your dream!' Dr King heard her, pushed his prepared notes to one side, and went on to speak extemporaneously for a further five minutes ... and to deliver one of the most memorable speeches in human history:

I say to you today, my friends, that in spite of the difficulties and frustrations of the moment, I still have a dream. It is a dream deeply rooted in the American dream. I have a dream that one day this nation will rise up and live out the true meaning of its creed: 'We hold these truths to be self-evident: that all men are created equal.'

I have a dream that one day on the red hills of Georgia the sons of former slaves and the sons of former slave owners will be able to sit down together at a table of brotherhood. I have a dream that one day even the state of Mississippi, a desert state, sweltering with the heat of injustice and oppression, will be transformed into an oasis of freedom and justice. I have a dream that my four little children will one day live in a nation where they will not be judged by the colour of their skin but by the content of their character. I have a dream today.

There was nothing 'infantile' or 'hallucinatory' about this dream. It was costly and daring, but it was also beautiful and true. Has Martin Luther King's dream been realised? Well, yes and no. There is still much racial prejudice, but just forty-six years after he made that speech, I, with much of the world, watched spellbound as America swore in its first *black* president.

You have a right to your dreams. You don't have a right to them all being fulfilled, and you don't have the right to crush other people in order to achieve them. But you have a right to stretch forward to the goals that are on your heart. And I would go further. I would say you have a duty – most of all to yourself – to see whether pursuing your dream – even one that may now be lying dormant – could change not just *your* world, but the lives and the world of others.

But dreamers sometimes have a difficult time; there is no shortage of people who are ready to pour cold water on our dreams. When I was fourteen I was really struggling at school – I often came near the bottom of the class. One day, as part of a careers guidance programme, our year was invited to visit an architect's office. As I got up from my desk to join some other kids who were going on the trip, my teacher shouted out, 'Where are you going, Parsons?' I replied, 'I may become an architect, sir.' He laughed out loud.

But it's not just the cold-water throwers who will try to put us off. Sometimes even our friends and family try to dissuade us from pursuing our dreams because they want to keep us from the pain of failure. I eventually became a lawyer, but when I told my father about my dream he said, 'People like us don't become solicitors.' Those who think like this don't understand that the greatest pain is not in failing, but in looking back when we are old and thinking, 'I should have tried.'

Let me tell you about a man called Charles Darrow, who lived in Pennsylvania. After losing his job in a sales company during the Great Wall Street Crash of 1929, Darrow tried to support his wife and child by carrying out various odd jobs like gardening and household repairs.

Darrow noticed that his neighbours and friends enjoyed playing a board game. There were several variations of it, and it involved buying and selling property. He decided to produce his own version of the game. Thinking back to when he lived in Atlantic City, he began to paint out its streets on the oilcloth that covered the kitchen table, and make little houses and other buildings out of wood. He continued developing his idea in his spare time until he was finally satisfied with the new game. He called it *Monopoly*.

Darrow and his family started to make up copies of the game at home, and soon he was selling them around the neighbourhood for four dollars each. He then offered a few sets to a Philadelphia department store and orders for the game grew so much that the point came when he had to make a decision about whether to manufacture the game on a full-scale basis himself, or sell the idea to a games company. He decided to approach Parker Brothers, the largest games manufacturer in the world.

The famous company's response was not promising. They rejected it, saying that the game had fundamental errors: it was far too complex and long – everyone knew that the maximum amount of time for a board game to hold the attention was forty-five minutes, whereas this game could go on for hours. Undaunted, and believing utterly in his invention, Darrow went to a local printer and ordered five thousand copies to be made up, agreeing to pay the bill as the games were sold. One of the stores who agreed to trial it was F. A. O. Schwartz in New York, and it was just before Christmas when one customer decided to buy this curious new game as a present for her games-mad husband. He loved it! Oh, and by the way, his name was Robert Barton – and he was the president of Parker Brothers.

Within weeks, Charles Darrow had been invited to New York by Robert Barton himself and was offered a very generous licensing agreement which he accepted. It made him an instant millionaire – in real money! The game has become Parker Brothers' (in the US) and Waddington's (outside the US) bestselling game of all time. Sales have topped two hundred and fifty million and there are an estimated five hundred million regular players around the world.

I sometimes wonder whether we find our dreams so hard to pursue because we simply cannot *imagine* them. When I was a small boy, I used to sit in front of the coal fire in our living room, gaze into the labyrinth of glowing ash and flame, and just . . . imagine. I wish I did more of that now. I think we too easily imprison imagination in the world of childhood.

Do we ever imagine? When we are going through tough times, can we imagine that life was different? Can we imagine our job was fulfilling, that we are reconciled with a friend, that we felt love for our husband or wife again, that our teenage child was more reasonable? Can we imagine our dream being fulfilled?

Sometimes it's difficult to imagine things being any different. That's not hard to understand; our very survival depends on us taking reality seriously. And yet a lack of the ability to imagine will tie us to the belief that life can never be different to how it is today. In 1798 Robert Thomas Malthus, who was the expert on population growth, was asked to report on the implications of everyone in London having access to their own form of personal transportation. He thought the prospect ridiculous: 'The streets of the metropolis would be fourteen feet deep in manure.' Any form of transport other than the horse was literally *unimaginable* for the great mathematician. (I think it's safe to say he never got hit by a car, but I like to imagine a prototype bicycle giving him a heck of a shock!)

Lack of imagination can be not only foolish but positively dangerous. When the findings of the 9/11 Commission into the 2001 terrorist attacks in the US were published, Chairman Thomas Kean commented that history would show that the greatest failure of the US intelligence services was not in policy, resources or management, but 'one of imagination'. The report concluded that the security services had operated within the boundaries of the 'known realm' and, as a result, had failed to anticipate that the methods used by al Qaeda on 9/11 would differ dramatically from those used in the past. The strongest recommendation of the report was that it was crucial 'to find ways of routinizing, even bureaucratizing, the exercise of the *imagination*'.

Imagination is important because it can open our minds to real possibilities – and therefore to solutions. Maybe we should take a leaf from the 9/11 report and 'routinize' imagining – build it in to our work programmes, our strategy forums, and even our family discussions.

Albert Einstein said, 'Imagination is more important than knowledge. For knowledge is limited to all we now know and understand, while imagination embraces the entire world, and all there ever will be to know and understand.'

So perhaps we shouldn't write off imagination too quickly, as though its only place is in the minds of children. Perhaps there's a kind of imagination that takes vision, courage, and even faith.

Go for your dreams – even if friends pour cold water on them, or you fail at first. Even if those dreams are not fulfilled, you will be able to look back later with the satisfaction of knowing that you gave it everything. There is joy in that.

Dale Carnegie said, 'Are you bored with life? Then throw yourself into some work you believe in with all your heart, live for it, die for it, and you will find happiness that you had thought could never be yours.'

I've already mentioned one American statesman, but let me end with something said by another one – Robert F. Kennedy: 'Some men see things as they are and ask "Why?" I dream things that never were and ask . . . "Why not?"'

P.S. If you are to see your dreams fulfilled, though, you are going to need an important quality: perseverance. We'll talk about it next time we meet.

5

Keep on keeping on

A COUPLE OF YEARS ago, I met a remarkable woman and heard her story of perseverance. I was about to give a keynote speech at a company's annual conference and was sitting in the front row waiting to take my turn at the podium. When the previous speaker finished, the room erupted in applause and the woman sitting next to me whispered in my ear, 'I bet you're not looking forward to following *her*.' As I left my seat I whispered back, 'Thanks for that great encouragement!' But she was right.

Liz had told us that she left school with just one GCSE, in Drama. She went to college to try some retakes, but failed them abysmally again. Eventually she got a job as a youth trainee in a business that conducted cold calling at a very high level. Their aim was to obtain appointments for their clients with the CEOs of major companies. Liz's job consisted of carrying out all the functions of an office junior. She wasn't very good at typing or admin, but her boss heard her on the phone once and suggested she tried her hand at making telephone calls. She was brilliant at it. Soon she had joined the telephone team permanently, and within a short time she was heading up her own department in the USA.

She was still only in her early twenties when she decided that she wanted to set up her own company in the UK. When she broke the news to her boss, he was thrilled for her and said that he would be her first client.

Liz approached a bank for a loan, but the bank said no. Eventually the Prince's Trust gave her a grant of £1000 and she started her business in her flat. And then, over a period of three months, Liz became completely blind. She'd had a progressive eye disease and her sight had gradually worsened over the years, always with the threat that she would lose it completely. And now it had happened . . . just as her dream of running her own business was getting underway.

After some time, she had a visit from some specialists whose aim was to help her decide how she could make a living now she was blind. She told them she was going to build a successful marketing company.

Liz said that when they heard about her plan the specialists explained about something called SMART goals, and told her to assess the likelihood of the success of her dream against these criteria. The 'S', they said, stood for 'specific' and they agreed that her plan met that condition. The 'M' was for 'measurable', a condition she also met – she had systems in place to measure her business's progress. 'A' stood for 'achievable', something that they regarded as unlikely, and 'R' was for 'realistic', a criterion which she certainly failed. 'T' was 'time related', and she was OK on that one, but overall she failed two out of the five SMART goals. Her dream could not succeed. Liz asked what she could do instead and they suggested that she either pursue a career in massage therapy, or become a piano tuner. Liz told us, 'I hate touching other people's bodies, and I haven't got a musical note in my head, so I told them I was going to build my marketing company anyway.'

When she stood in front of us that day, Liz Jackson was the Managing Director of Great Guns Marketing, which has now become the UK's leading business-to-business telemarketing agency. She is also Managing Director of Talk Telematics, a gold partner reseller for TomTom, which has an outstanding collection of business awards. Liz herself was given the Young Businesswoman of the Year award, was honoured by the Queen with an MBE in

2007 for services to business, and has appeared on Channel 4's *Secret Millionaire* programme. She ended her talk like this: 'Ladies and gentlemen, SMART goals are pants! Sometimes we need dreams!'

Liz Jackson is right; but as she discovered, the problem with dreams is that the world is full of 'dream killers'. These characters go around carrying a large bucket filled with very cold water in the hope of meeting somebody who will tell them about their ambition. Just take a look at some of these famous ones from history.

'There is no reason for any individual to have a computer in their home.'

– Kenneth Olsen,
president and founder of Digital Equipment
Corporation, 1977

'Airplanes are interesting toys but of no military value.'

– Marshal Ferdinand Foch,
French military strategist, 1911

'Man will never reach the moon regardless of all future scientific advances.'

– Dr Lee De Forest,
inventor of the Audion tube and father of radio, 1967

'[Television] won't be able to hold onto any market it captures after the first six months. People will soon get tired of staring at a plywood box every night.'

> – Darryl F. Zanuck,
> head of Twentieth Century Fox, 1946

'We don't like their sound and guitar music is on the way out.'

> – Decca Recording Company executive
> rejecting The Beatles, 1962

'This 'telephone' has too many shortcomings to be seriously considered as a means of communications. The device is inherently of no value to us.'

> – Western Union internal memo, 1876

'Everything that can be invented has been invented.'

> – Charles H. Duell,
> US Commissioner of Patents, 1899

Imagine that you were a young Steve Jobs (the founder of Apple) in 1977 and you'd decided to share your dream about putting computers in every home with Kenneth Olsen – you'd have got soaked! But these dream killers are not confined to history. You will find them around today – in schools, colleges, offices and homes. I have no idea what your dreams in life will be, but I know this: you don't have a *right* to fulfil them, but you do have a right to *try* to do so. And normally one round of trying isn't enough; we have to try again and *again*.

Liz Jackson told us that even after she went blind she was motivated to press on with her dream because of something that her father used to say to her time and time again when she was a child. It came from the lips of Henry Ford: 'If you think you can or you think you can't – you're absolutely right.'

Let me tell you another story to illustrate this. It was 7 p.m. on 20 October 1968 in the Olympic Stadium in Mexico City. The light was beginning to fade and the temperature was finally starting to cool. The closing ceremonies had just finished and the athletes and spectators were beginning to leave the stadium when they heard the sound of wailing police sirens. Those who were high up in the stands could see motorcycles with flashing blue lights surrounding someone who was making his way towards the stadium. Whoever it was, they were moving very slowly.

By the time the police escort got to the gates, the public address announcer said that a final marathon runner was making his way into the arena. The crowd was confused. Over an hour earlier Mamo Wolde of Ethiopia had charged across the finish line to win the marathon. What had taken this last runner so long? The first sight of him as he came through the tunnel wearing the colours of Tanzania told the story. John Stephen Akhwari's leg was bandaged and bloody – he had taken a bad fall early in the race, was trampled on, dislocated his knee and hit his shoulder hard on the ground. Now, nearly twenty-six miles later, it was all he could do to limp his way around the track. The crowd stood and encouraged Akhwari through the last few yards of his race with an ovation that far exceeded the one given to the man who had come in first. When he crossed the finish line, he collapsed into the arms of paramedics who immediately rushed him to hospital.

The next day a journalist asked him the question on everyone's lips: why, after sustaining the kinds of injuries he had, did he get up and carry on with the race when there was no way he could win a medal? Akhwari's reply was this: 'My country did not send me five thousand miles to Mexico City to start the race. They sent me five thousand miles to finish it.'

6

Love is something you do

IWONDER IF YOU will be married when you read this. If I miss your wedding, and if it's possible to regret things from beyond the grave, that's one thing I will be sad about. If I do get to go along, though, I'm sure I will embarrass you – I'll tell crummy jokes to your friends, try to dance, insist on making a speech, and lose my notes and my glasses.

Wedding days are special for so many reasons, but most of all, perhaps, because they are full not just of love, but of hope. Of course, in so many ways the day is perfect. The bride always looks beautiful and the groom looks as good as he's ever going to look in the whole of his life. We are the centre of attention – and deeply in love.

Feeling in love is a wonderful sensation. I remember

when I first held your grandmother's hand, a tingle went up my spine. And when I kissed her on Christmas Eve in 1964, the snow was on her hair and her lips were warm. You've got a hot grandmother.

In fact the *feeling* of love is so good that many of us make the mistake of confusing it with love itself. If we make that error, then when the feeling dies down, or even goes for a while, we assume that love has died. But if you are to know love that really lasts over the long haul – whether it is with your partner, your friend, or your child – you are going to have to go on loving when you don't *feel* like it.

When I got married, five years after the day I kissed your grandmother with the snow in her hair, the preacher read out a passage from the Bible. Some people think it is the greatest definition of love in the world. Here's a little of what it says: 'Love is patient, love is kind. It does not envy . . . it is not self-seeking, it is not easily angered, it keeps no record of wrongs.'*

It was many years later before I realised that those words actually described love as a way of living with somebody else that involved choices that had to be made every day. It was a big shock when it dawned on me that if I was going to go on loving your grandmother, I would

* 1 Corinthians 13:4–5 NIV.

sometimes have to put what I wanted in second place. I would need to make sure I did little acts of kindness so that she could not only hear me say I loved her, but *see* it. I'd have to make a better effort to bite my tongue. Marriage was not so much about feeling, but about *doing* love.

Let me say right now that none of us wants to be in a relationship where it is all duty and no emotion – and no matter what people say, it's not always possible to keep relationships together. But of this I am sure: unless we learn to go on loving when the romantic feelings of love seem to have faded, we will never experience a long-term love with anybody. And for that very reason there are times when love has to be not so much an affair of the heart, but of the *will*.

Louis de Bernière's *Captain Corelli's Mandolin** is one of the British public's best-loved novels, and the film was a blockbuster. It is set on the Greek island of Cephalonia during the Italian and German occupation of the Second World War. One of the main characters is Pelagia, the daughter of the local physician, Dr Iannis. She is helplessly in love with Antonio Corelli, an Italian army captain. In one of the most moving scenes of the film Dr Iannis explains to his daughter the nature of real love.

* Louis de Bernières, *Captain Corelli's Mandolin* (Vintage, 1998).

When you fall in love it is a temporary madness. It erupts like an earthquake, and then it subsides. And when it subsides, you have to make a decision. You have to work out whether your roots are to become so entwined together that it is inconceivable that you should ever part. Because this is what love is. Love is not breathlessness, it is not excitement . . . It is not lying awake at night imagining that he is kissing every part of your body . . . For that is just being in love, which any of us can convince ourselves we are. Love itself is what is left over when being in love has burned away.

Over a lifetime of writing and speaking about some of these issues I have never found a better illustration of that kind of loving – not just with the heart but with the will – than something that was written by Dr Richard Selzer, a surgeon:

I stand by the bed where a young woman lies, her face post-operative, her mouth twisted in palsy, clownish. A tiny twig of the facial nerve, the one to the muscles of her mouth, has been severed. She will be thus from now on. The surgeon has followed with religious fervour, the curve of her flesh, I promise you that. Nevertheless, to remove the tumour in her cheek, I have cut a little nerve. Her young husband is in the room. He stands on the opposite side of the bed and together they seem to dwell in the evening lamp light, isolated from me, private. 'Who are they,' I ask myself, 'he and this wry mouth that I have made, who gaze at and touch each other so greedily?' The young woman speaks. 'Will my mouth always be like this?' she asks. 'Yes it will,' I say. 'It is because the nerve was cut.' She nods and is silent, but the young man smiles, 'I like it,' he says, 'it's kind of cute.' And all at once, I know who he is and I lower my gaze. One is not bold in an encounter with a god. And unmindful I see he bends to kiss her crooked mouth, and I so close, I can see how he twists his own lips to accommodate to hers, to show their kiss still works. And I remember that the gods appeared in ancient times as mortals and I hold my breath, and let the wonder in.*

I wonder why that incident impacted this surgeon so strongly that he wrote of its power years later. I think it is simply because it is a demonstration of love in action.

* Richard Selzer, *Mortal Lessons: Notes on the Art of Surgery*, reprint (Harcourt Brace, 1996).

Life had not turned out as the young man had thought, and the truth was that his wife was not as attractive now as when he married her. But what changed in him was not just in the shape of his lips; it was a change in the depths of his being as he took a *decision* not only to go on loving, but to go on *accepting*.

In almost every relationship there will come a time when our partner becomes unattractive to us – whether physically or emotionally – and it may seem then that we have fallen out of love. It is especially easy to feel that way if we have met somebody else for whom we have begun to experience the kinds of love *feelings* that we knew when we first met our partner. This is the most crucial time of any relationship: it is the moment when we have to decide whether we are prepared to say 'I *will* love you' even if, at that time, our feelings seem to tell us otherwise. Sometimes couples do this for what they call 'the sake of the kids'. It's not always the right reason, but it is still a good reason. And for whatever reason they do it, there are countless couples who have, in the process of changing the shape of their lips, rekindled a love they thought was gone for ever.

Their kiss still worked.

was already a hundred and fifty years old when she came

7

Saul's armour

WHEN I WAS a child my parents didn't go to church,
but one cold January day, when I was about four
years old, there was a knock on the door of our tiny ter-
raced house. My mother answered it. It was Miss Williams,
the Sunday school teacher from the little church on the
corner of our street. She asked my mother whether there
were any children in the house who would like to go to
Sunday school. I don't really know whether it was concern
for my spiritual welfare or the prospect of some free
childcare, but apparently my mother didn't hesitate. She
pointed at me and said, 'He'd like to go.'

And so Miss Williams took me by the hand and led me
down the street and into the world of Sunday school. Fifty
years later I was asked to speak at the one-hundredth

anniversary of that little church. As I was leaving, some-body pulled my sleeve. I turned and a voice said, 'Do you remember me?' It was Miss Williams. I only just stopped myself from saying, 'You're still alive!' I had thought she was already a hundred and ten years old when she came to my house for me on that first winter's day!

Miss Williams died a few years ago. She was never actually a mother to children of her own, but in truth she had hundreds of kids. And she had two wonderful qualities. The first is not an attribute that is mentioned much these days. In fact, it almost seems to belong to another age, but it is a truly lovely trait. Miss Williams was *kind*. I'm not sure I can adequately explain that char-acteristic, except to say that she seemed to have no personal agenda, nothing to prove, and to be genuinely more interested in you than she was in herself. But it is only on looking back that I've realised how very kind she was, because at the time it was her second quality for which we children really loved her: she was a won-derful raconteur. At three o'clock on a Sunday afternoon we would cram into the little classroom, and Miss Williams would tell us stories.

And what stories they were – lions and battles, arks and miracles! She told them with so much passion and mystery that years later, when I went to the West End to see *Joseph and the Amazing Technicolor Dreamcoat*, I couldn't help but think that the director could have learned a trick or two from my old Sunday school teacher.

One story she loved to tell was about a young shepherd boy called David who decided that he was going to fight a giant called Goliath. Miss Williams told us that, humanly speaking, David didn't stand a chance. The giant was covered in armour, had a massive spear, a shield and I don't know what else. All David had was a slingshot, a few stones that he took out of a brook, and 'faith in God', as she would tell us.

Even now, almost sixty years later, I feel I can still hear Miss Williams describe the flight of the stone as it left the shepherd boy's sling. I can hear the shocked gasps of the kids as that stone embedded itself into Goliath's forehead. And I can see the wide eyes all around me as David cut off Goliath's head with the giant's own sword. As I recall this, I'm thinking that perhaps it's just as well Miss Williams has departed this life. If she hadn't, perhaps social services would be knocking on her door any day now.

I suppose that, at least among the boys, David and Goliath was our favourite story. Most of us kids felt an affinity with the underdog and had at least one school bully in mind whom we wouldn't mind decapitating. Yes, Miss Williams was a great storyteller, and from the day I first heard that epic from her lips, many years were to pass until a dreadful realisation dawned on me: in one respect at least in the telling of this story, Miss Williams was *wrong*.

Now I wouldn't bother telling you this just to say that my Sunday school teacher wasn't infallible. I'm doing so because I believe that if you can grasp *why* she was wrong, it might just change your life someday. Do you remember that I said Miss Williams always portrayed David as the underdog? It's not hard to understand why she did, but historian Robert Dohrenwend begs to differ. He says, 'Goliath had as much chance against David as any Bronze Age warrior with a sword would have had against an [opponent] armed with a .45 pistol.'* Giving further weight to this take on the matter, in his recent book *David and Goliath: Underdogs, Misfits and The Art of Battling Giants*, Malcolm Gladwell writes:

> Eitan Hirsch, a ballistics expert . . . recently did a series of calculations showing that a typical-size stone hurled by an expert slinger at a distance of thirty-five meters would have hit Goliath's head with a velocity of thirty-four meters per second – more than enough to penetrate his skull and render him unconscious or dead. In terms of stopping

* Robert E. Dohrenwend, PhD, 'The Sling: Forgotten firepower of antiquity', *Journal of Asian Martial Arts*, vol. 11, no. 2, 2002, pp. 28–49.

power, that is equivalent to a fair-size modern handgun.*

I can well imagine that right now you are wondering how this bit of information is actually meant to change your life. Well, it is simply this: you have to have the courage to do what David did: to play to your strengths and have faith in your own gifts and abilities. When David asked King Saul's permission to fight the giant, the king agreed and gave David his own armour to wear. But the second David put all that stuff on he knew he had made a dreadful mistake – he could hardly move.

Both Saul and Goliath assumed that David was going to take part in one-on-one combat – an ancient ritual that allowed the results of battle to be decided by the death of one man instead of hundreds. But David had no intention of doing that any more than he had fancied one-on-one combat with the bear or the lion that he had killed with his sling. As David took off Saul's armour he said, in essence: 'I cannot wear your armour because I am not you. If you allow me to be me and let me use the talents God has given me, then both you and Goliath will have an almighty shock.' And with that he picked up a

* Malcolm Gladwell, *David and Goliath: Underdogs, Misfits and The Art of Battling Giants* (Allen Lane, 2013).

small leather pouch that was attached to two strands of rope.

Malcolm Gladwell explains why, in the right hands, the sling was such a devastating weapon:

> They would put a rock or a lead ball into the pouch, swing it around in increasingly wider and faster circles, and then release one end of the rope, hurling the rock forward . . . Paintings from medieval times show slingers hitting birds in midflight . . . and in the Book of Judges, slingers are described as being accurate to 'within a hair's breadth' . . . The Romans even had a special set of tongs made just to remove stones that had been embedded in some poor soldier's body by a sling.

Goliath yelled at David, 'Come to me.' He was gearing himself up for a close-quarters fight. But David had no intention of getting any nearer – at least not until the giant was horizontal. Goliath watched as the young boy put a stone in his sling and aimed at his forehead, the only unprotected part of his body. And maybe he suddenly understood, with terror, why David didn't look scared. Goliath's day was about to get a whole lot worse.

The world is full of people who will want you to do things just like them: they will push you into jobs for which you're not suited, make you run races you have no chance of winning, or give you strategies that in your hands will probably fail; in short, they will want you to wear Saul's armour. Now, of course, sometimes it's good to be pushed out of your comfort zone – but don't make a lifestyle out of it. As you politely take their armour off, turn to what comes naturally – to what you are gifted at – and have confidence in that.

Before I close, let me take you to another scene where a young man is facing his giant. First, though, we have to go back to 1998, when England was playing Argentina, trying to qualify for the World Cup quarter finals. David Beckham had been fouled by Diego Simione and was lying on the ground. As Simione went past him, Beckham kicked him lightly in the calf. Simione went down as though he had been hit by a truck. He later said that he was actively trying to get Beckham sent off. The Argentinian players surrounded the referee and demanded that Beckham go. He was given a red card. Down to ten men, England could only manage a draw and were duly ejected from the World Cup.

To say that Beckham became the target of vitriol and abuse from England supporters would be a gross under-statement. An effigy was made of him and hung on a gallows outside a London pub. The *Mirror* newspaper printed a dartboard with his face as the bull's-eye and invited readers to vent their anger. He received several death threats. It must have felt to him that he was hated by the whole nation. He was twenty-three years old.

Now fast-forward three years. It is 2001 and England's World Cup qualifying match against Greece. It is the ninety-third minute and England is trailing 2:1. If the score stays that way England will be out of the competition. There is an infringement just outside the Greek penalty area. I have no idea what went through Beckham's mind at that moment. On the one hand, the sensible thing to do might have been to let somebody else take the kick. It was likely to be the last one of the match and it was quite far out, with a wall of Greek defenders between the ball and the goal. Missing this one would hardly endear him any more to the England supporters.

But stronger than those understandable feelings of fear, I think Beckham had the belief that, succeed or fail, this would be a defining moment for him. Like David of old he had the opportunity to face his giant armed only with his own intrinsic skill. This is how Beckham described what happened in those moments:

I could hear the banging of a drum. It was as if it was the only sound in the world. Just one drum, banging out a beat, the sound carrying directly onto the pitch. The rest of the stadium seemed completely silent, as if every single fan knew that the next kick of the ball would decide the match.

Bang, bang; bang, bang; bang, bang.

Teddy Sheringham, my England team-mate, tried to pick up the ball and place it on the spot where Emile Heskey had been fouled by a Greek defender a few moments earlier. I felt a rush of adrenaline . . . Unless we scored now, we wouldn't qualify for the 2002 World Cup.

It didn't bear thinking about.

I grabbed the ball away from Teddy and replaced it myself. He wasn't too keen on my interference. He shoulder-barged me away, gently but firmly. 'I've got this, David,' he said. 'I know I can make it.'

But nothing was going to stop me taking that free kick. I felt confident, calm, certain . . .

'It's too far out for you, Teddy,' I said. 'Trust me. I've got it' . . .

Teddy could see that I was not going to back down and, even though he was older and wiser than me, he stepped away. It was just me, the ball, and the twenty-five yards separating me from the top left corner of the goal.

But this kick was not just about England; it was also about me. It was about drawing a line under four years of abuse. Four years of bitterness.

Four years of England fans – not all of them, but enough to make it hurt – shouting the most horrible things at me while I was playing for my country.

Four years of pain.*

The sense of silence in the stadium was not just there, it was in mansions and council houses, and pubs and clubs across the country as people sat immobile in front of their televisions. Beckham let fly and at first it seemed he had misjudged it – and then that incredible bend kicked in. A fine, but hapless Greek goalkeeper watched as if in slow motion as the ball nestled itself in the top left-hand corner of his net.

A nation exploded with raw emotion.

I'm a football fan. I've seen lots of free kicks in my time, some of them more impressive than Beckham's on that day. But I have never forgotten the sheer thrill of watching somebody with such an understanding of the one thing in life that they could do best – and with the courage to use that gift, even if the result was failure. I think I might have felt the same if I'd been seeing a young boy with a sling walk slowly down the hill of the Elah Valley towards the giant who taunted him.

But Beckham didn't discover or develop that gift on his own. His father, and Alex Ferguson, and no doubt a number of other people unknown except to Beckham himself, helped that boy not only hone his gift but *believe in it*. And for that reason I'd urge you to search out mentors in your life – teachers, coaches, employers, friends even – who are bright enough not to want to dump Saul's armour on you, but to help you discover the strengths and talents that are in *you*.

And if you do, you will find that your giants fall faster.

8

Be the change

IS THERE SOMETHING in your life you'd like to change? When you read this, you could be married or single, have children, be wealthy or poor, have a job or be seeking work. Of course, I have no way of knowing, but let me imagine that you are married. I wonder – do you ever catch yourself wishing that your partner was more fun to be with, or perhaps slimmer or sexier? If you have children, do you wish that one of them was more like the other – maybe that they were more academic, more reliable, or that they handled money more carefully? And what about your friends – say, your best friend? Do you wish that they were different in some way – that they didn't have *that* annoying characteristic, perhaps? What about your neighbours? In a perfect world, whose door would you love to see the furniture removal van draw up at?

A few years before you were born, one of the main political parties in the United Kingdom came up with an election slogan they thought would really get people's attention: 'It's Time for Change!' In theory, the slogan should have worked pretty well – it's an incredibly powerful message. It strikes at the inner chord of dissatisfaction that people have with their lives, their workplaces, their communities and their world. We see things that irritate us and things that make us downright angry and we demand change. But the campaign failed. I wonder why. Perhaps it was because the electorate knew that, too often, change isn't all it's cracked up to be. And as the French proverb says, *Plus ça change, plus c'est la même chose* – the more things change, the more they stay the same.

But perhaps it failed for another reason: perhaps the electorate is brighter than politicians think. Perhaps, in our hearts, we know that if we can't bring about change in our own family, street or workplace, there's not much chance that a bunch of strangers in the middle of London is going to be able to change our world.

I think that's absolutely true. Mahatma Gandhi said, 'We must become the change we want to see in others.' Real change is never successfully imposed from without, but must be inspired from within. Barak Obama said,

'Change will not come if we wait for some other person or some other time. We are the ones we've been waiting for. We are the change that we seek.'

If you have never read it, can I encourage you to get a copy of *The Diary of a Young Girl* by Anne Frank?* In July 1942, trying to escape the horrors of Nazi death camps, Anne Frank and her Jewish family hid in the attic of an Amsterdam warehouse. Anne was just thirteen years old. For two years she lived in a confined area with seven other people. They were cold, hungry and in constant fear of discovery. Her diary ends abruptly in August 1944 when the group were discovered. Anne died in the Bergen-Belsen concentration camp just a few months before liberation.

What makes her diary so remarkable is Anne's unshakeable courage and optimism when confronted with terror. Here are a few extracts:

If I just think of how we live here, I usually come to the conclusion that it is a paradise compared with how other Jews who are not in hiding must be living. (Saturday, 1 May 1943)

I've found that there is always some beauty left in nature, sunshine, freedom, in yourself; these can all

---

* Anne Frank, *The Diary of a Young Girl* (first published 1947).

help you. Look at these things, then you find yourself again, and God, and then you regain your balance. And whoever is happy will make others happy too. He who has courage and faith will never perish in misery! (Tuesday, 7 March 1944)

It's really a wonder that I haven't dropped all my ideals, because they seem so absurd and impossible to carry out. Yet I keep them, because in spite of everything I still believe that people are really good at heart. I simply can't build up my hopes on a foundation consisting of confusion, misery, and death. (Saturday, 15 July 1944)

It is incredible to think that if this young girl were alive today she would still be only eighty-five years old. Anne's life may have been terrifyingly short, but she has left a legacy which has already inspired generations, and will go on doing so. In 1999 she was identified by *Time* magazine as one of the one hundred most influential people of the twentieth century. Her diary is the bestselling of all time.

Although, in one sense she will be remembered as yet another *victim* of the Holocaust, in a different sense her courage and belief ensured that she will be remembered as a *victor* over it. If a teenage girl can rise in such a sublime way above such unspeakable evil, who are we to deny that we cannot do the same with our own challenges? In the midst of the most difficult circumstances, Anne Frank decided to *become the change*. In her final days in the attic she wrote, 'How wonderful it is that nobody need wait a single moment before starting to improve the world.'

A friend of mine is a politician. When he was first elected, he was very keen to impress his constituents with his commitment to his locality and his efficiency in bringing about change. But he found one constituent particularly difficult to please. The man would write almost every month complaining about the state of the small patch of grass outside his front boundary wall; it was full of weeds, and he demanded that the council do something about it. My friend did his best to get the matter sorted, but the combination of his being a new boy on the block and the minor nature of the constituent's request meant that the council never did get that piece of gardening done.

One Saturday morning, after ploughing through yet another missive from his constituent, my friend had an idea. Later that day he called at the man's house. He introduced himself and asked the man to accompany him outside into the street. The patch of grass had been weeded to perfection. The constituent was elated and told my friend that he was a brilliant politician. The man asked him how he had managed to get the council to 'get off their backsides and get it done'. My friend replied, 'I didn't. I did it myself this afternoon. It took me twenty minutes.' The man was incandescent with rage.

I wonder why. Perhaps it was the obvious implication that he himself could easily have brought about the change he so desperately wanted. If 'It's Time for Change' is to become a force for change in society instead of merely an election slogan, change has to start with each of us.

The really sobering truth is that, usually, you can't change another person – not your husband or wife, your friend, your boss or your next-door neighbour. You can only change yourself – the way you speak to them, the way you appreciate them and tell them so, the way you try to figure out what they might like to see changed in you. And sometimes, because change is a dynamic thing, when we change, other people change as well. The only alternative is to *actually* change them – oh, not their personalities, but the people themselves. You must find a new husband or wife, a new boss, some new friends who are more to your liking . . . and be sure to move away from that difficult neighbour.

But first, can I suggest you at least try the other way? There are no guarantees that people will respond positively – but try it. Try speaking to your partner with more affection, try expressing appreciation to those you love, tell your friends that you value them, and start saying 'good morning' to that neighbour you haven't spoken to in years. You never know, one day you might just get a 'good morning' back, and the day you do, you will have begun to change the world – *your world.*

9

No regrets

L AST YEAR I got off a plane in Johannesburg, switched
on my mobile phone and saw a text message asking
me to ring home immediately. I made the call during the
short bus ride from the plane to the terminal and discovered that my good and dear friend, Bob, had died in his
sleep. His death was both sudden and unexpected: he was
not old, nor, to my knowledge, ill. I bent over in a corner
of Baggage Reclaim and cried helplessly.

Bob was a builder. Yes, I know what you're thinking
– and he enjoyed the joke as well. And there were other
smiles with Bob: when you showed him a job you wanted
done, he would always go through the same routine. He
would look around the room, stare up at the ceiling,
examine the walls, go outside, look at the roof, and then

he would purse his lips, suck in a breath of air and say, 'Who did this work for you? It's terrible!'

I would reply, '*You* did, Bob.'

And he would blush, shrug his shoulders and say, 'Ah, well, it was a long time ago . . .'

Four of us used to play snooker together. The most you can score in a snooker match is one hundred and forty-seven – only achieved by potting all the reds and every colour in the right order. On the wall of the snooker room was a chalkboard where we kept a record of the highest score ever achieved among us. That figure had not changed for almost five years: 35. When I returned from South Africa I went to the room where we used to play and noticed that after our last game Bob had sneaked back and written on the chalkboard: 'Bob – 146'. Was he just too humble to claim a perfect score? I'll never know, but I decided that Bob's little joke will never be erased.

I was overwhelmed with grief and although I cried a lot, I almost felt as if I should have been crying more. I found myself shaking my head in disbelief. Sometimes I could almost hear him. On one occasion I rang his mobile phone just to hear his voice on the answer phone. I half expected him to saunter into the snooker room one night and say, 'You are doomed in this game! I've brought my new snooker cue with me.' Even some weeks afterwards, I actually pinched myself to be sure it wasn't some dreadful nightmare from which I could mercifully wake. In C. S. Lewis's *A Grief Observed*, Lewis deals with the fact that grief often comes in waves – and keeps coming. He puts it like this:

> [i]n grief nothing 'stays put'. One keeps on emerging from a phase, but it always recurs . . . Will it be for always? How often will the vast emptiness astonish me like a complete novelty and make me say, 'I never realized my loss until this moment?' . . . They say the coward dies many times; so does the beloved.*

People said to me, 'Time will heal.' But that's not true. Time does makes the loss easier, but it doesn't heal. It's not meant to heal. The truth is that as the years go by we find what some call a 'new normal' – a way of living without the one we have loved so much – but the pain never goes completely.

After Bob died, I knew that there would be no quick fix for my grief, but I did have at least one consolation: there were no regrets. I would not have been able to say that about every friend who died suddenly, but I *was* able to say it about Bob. Did we ever hurt each other? Yes – but like a grouchy old couple, we eventually made up. Did

---

* C. S. Lewis, *A Grief Observed* (first published by Faber & Faber, 1961).

we take time to simply laugh together? Yes – I have a hundred memories of silliness. But perhaps, above all, we told each other now and then how much we mattered to each other.

Later that year, I spoke to five hundred men at a conference. I told them about Bob and I urged them to tell their friends that they were appreciated and valued – loved even. As the words came out of my mouth I realised that it was an unusual thing to say to a bunch of men. But perhaps not so very strange: G. K. Chesterton said, 'The meanest fear is the fear of sentimentality.' George Eliot wrote, 'I like not only to be loved, but also to be told that I am loved . . . the realm of silence is large enough beyond the grave.'

Following the 9/11 terrorist attacks on the World Trade Center in New York, researchers analysed the phone calls made from the burning towers, and when they read the hurriedly sent emails and listened to the messages left on answering machines, they discovered that the same three words came up time and time again. They were not about bonuses or salary sizes; they didn't mention promotions or share prices. No. The same three words were said by lovers to lovers, wives to husbands, husbands to wives, parents to kids, friends to friends: 'I love you.'

This should not be a surprise to anyone because when it comes down to it, the thing that matters most to us in life is relationships. It's just that in all the busyness, we can sometimes forget that. And, perhaps even sadder still, when we do remember it, we don't actually *say* it.

Just yesterday one of you said, 'I love you, Pops,' not just once but three times over! Sometimes, as we get older, we find those expressions of love harder to make. I know not everyone is the emotional kind, but trust me on this, whether it's to a husband or wife, a partner, parent, child or friend, you won't regret moving out of your comfort zone so that you not only *feel* love for someone, but *tell* them so.

Just don't leave it too late.

10

Just do it

I T'S NEW YEAR'S Eve and it's time for some resolutions! Or is it? One wit said that the best way to
keep New Year resolutions is in a drawer in our desk.
Perhaps the problem with resolutions is that we often
spend more time *talking about* them than actually doing
them.

I don't know what goals you have in life at present,
either for the short or the longer term – it could be to run
a marathon, give up smoking or learn Spanish. But here's
a question for you: do you think you have more chance
of reaching these goals if you let a friend know about
them, or less? Well, the obvious answer is 'more', but you
might be wrong – at least according to a talk I have just
listened to by Derek Sivers at the TED Global 2010

Conference.* He says that if you tell somebody else your goal it is *less* likely that you will achieve it. When our friends acknowledge the goal, our minds enjoy the approval and tick the task off as 'done'. We are fooled into feeling satisfied – whereas if we keep it to ourselves it gnaws away at our subconscious and prods us on to achieving it. This risk was first suggested in 1928 by Kurt Lewin, often recognised as the founder of social psychology. He called it 'substitution', or in Sivers' words, 'Your mind mistakes the talking for the doing.'

I don't know whether Sivers is right or wrong, but I do know that it's very easy to talk a lot about doing things without actually taking even the first step towards seeing our ambition fulfilled. I remember exactly an occasion when I had been complaining to a friend about an aspect of my life that I wished was different. To be honest, I can't really remember what it was; it might have been my full in-tray, my attitude to somebody I found difficult, or my waistline. My friend wasn't a psychologist – I'd probably have got off more lightly if he had been. He listened, sighed as if he'd heard all this a hundred times before, and then made a very simple comment: 'If you don't change anything, then everything will be just the same.'

* TED Global 2010, www.ted.com/talks/derek_sivers_keep_your_goals_to_yourself [accessed 12 May 2014].

I have discovered that my friend is right. In themselves, wishes, hopes and good intentions don't change things. I mean, just consider the waistline thing. I don't know if you know this, but your great-grandfather was a postman. He walked miles, every day. One day when I was visiting him, he asked me, 'What do you do in that gym thing you've joined?'

'I walk, Dad,' I replied.

'Where do you walk?'

I coughed and muttered, 'I don't walk anywhere, Dad – it's just on a treadmill.'

Now your great-grandfather didn't have a sarcastic bone in his body, which made his next question even more annoying: 'Why don't you walk outside in the street?' Before I could summon up an answer he enquired further: 'What else do you do at the gym?'

I knew before I opened my mouth where this was going. 'I ride a bike, Dad.'

My father was on a roll: 'Where do you ride it?'

I was cross now and answered him rather brusquely: 'I don't ride anywhere, Dad – it's just on a machine.'

My father's eyebrows raised: 'How much do you pay to be a member of this gym thing?'

'Thirty pounds a month, Dad,' I spluttered.

His eyebrows went higher: 'And how often do you go there?'

I sighed deeply and whispered, 'When I started, I used to go three times a week. Now I might go once a month.'

Dad smiled. 'If I owned that gym thing, I'd arrange for my office window to look out on the path to the front door, and when you started to walk along it I'd shout out, "Quick! Look! Here comes the mug who pays us £360 a year to walk nowhere and cycle nowhere."'

You must forgive your great-grandfather. He was unsophisticated. He didn't understand gyms. He didn't realise that you don't actually have to *go* to the gym, because body fat is scared of direct debits and as soon as a monthly entry goes through your bank statement the pounds fall off straight away. He thought you actually had to walk a little, run a few miles and lift some weights to make a difference.

Some years ago a friend urged me to actually write down my goals, both personal and professional. And then he suggested that at least once a week I ask myself this question: 'Have I done anything in the last seven days that has moved me closer to seeing that goal achieved?'

I wonder what goals you have. Let's say you want to learn to speak Japanese. If so, are you the kind of person who looks up some language courses online this week, places an order for one of them and actually starts to learn Japanese next week, then spends at least some time struggling with strange syntax over the next few weeks and months? Or will you still be meeting friends at parties in twenty years' time and saying, 'I think I'll learn Japanese one day . . .'

There is a fascinating book tucked away in the middle of the Old Testament called Ecclesiastes – it is literally a 'wisdom' book. The *News of the World* newspaper (now defunct) used to have the by-line, 'All human life is here' – well, that's certainly true of Ecclesiastes. Near the beginning there is one of the most famous poems in the world. It starts with the two great certainties of individual life: 'There is a time for everything . . . a time to be born and a time to die.' It ends with the two certainties of international life: 'a time for peace and a time for war'. And in an age when we are dominated by the question 'How?' ('How can we solve this problem?' 'How can we achieve success?' 'How can I be happy?'), this ancient book asks us to consider another word: 'Why?'

But although Ecclesiastes often concerns itself with the meaning of life, it holds plenty of wisdom for the everyday issues we all have to deal with. And it has some advice about the dreams that have been hidden away for years in the understairs cupboard of our minds. You know the one – the project that you have been planning to start for ages, but the time was never quite right. It says, 'Whoever watches the wind will not plant; whoever looks at the clouds will not reap.' As long as we are afraid that the wind will blow our seed away, we will keep it safe in the barn of our inner life. It is true that the seed is not exposed to unknown risks, but its death, although slow, is as certain as if we had stamped on it the day we first had it – year by year, its vitality will slowly seep away. In other words, there may never be a perfect time to start sowing the seed of our idea. Sometimes you just have to stick the thing in the ground and see what happens.

And that's just another way of saying that if you don't change anything, then everything will be just the same. So whether it's asking that gorgeous person for a date, beginning the personal fitness programme, changing careers or starting a business, sometimes you have to stop worrying . . .

. . . and *just do it.*

II

The great bank robbery

I HOPE THAT YOU never get into debt – the kind of debt that keeps you awake at night. I have. I hadn't been married long, and I think I just got carried away with the ease of borrowing money. I remember coming downstairs early one morning when it was still dark, sitting at the kitchen table, crying and thinking, 'How on earth am I going to get out of this mess?'

If it ever happens to you, here are a few things I'd like you to try to remember. The first is that you are not alone. Plenty of other people have been there and come out the other side. Second, there is plenty of good free advice available about what to do, so don't pay other people to get you out of debt – too often they make things worse. Third, no matter what people may try to tell you, don't believe that you can borrow your way out of debt. The only long-term way to get out of debt for ever is to spend less than you earn.

But although it is true that we must each take personal responsibility if we do get into debt, nevertheless the financial institutions that undergird our society also sometimes let us down. Indulge an old man and allow me to tell you about something that happened a few years before you were born. It will certainly happen again sometime, and if you are around when it does, then knowing what occurred last time may help you and your family.

The reasons why it came about are complicated, but there is no doubt that a big part of it was a cataclysmic failure in the way our banks and building societies were monitored and run. Between 2008 and 2014, a severe economic recession swept across the USA and Europe. In the Great Depression of the 1930s, people who had lost all their money were jumping off skyscrapers. In this more recent depression, it was more like *governments* were jumping off skyscrapers! The mighty USA tottered on the brink, Greece, Italy, Spain and Ireland all had to be bailed out, and by the time you are reading this letter it is likely that the UK will still be repaying the money it borrowed to get out of trouble.

Of course, I have no way of knowing how interested you are in all this financial stuff, but before you start drifting off into a daydream, let me just give you a quick warning. It is this: at some point in your life you will almost certainly be part of a bank robbery. And it won't be your mugshot that's featured on *Crimewatch*, because you will be the victim. *Your bank will rob you.*

Sit back and let me tell you what happened in the early 2000s. Banks started lending money to just about anybody. All was well as long as the borrowers made the repayments. But eventually it became apparent that many of them couldn't. The house of cards started to totter, and then the banks themselves started to collapse.

Now governments don't like banks collapsing – it causes havoc in society. So most governments chose to give huge sums of money to the banks to help them survive. They borrowed most of that money from countries that hadn't been as stupid as their own. But then that debt got so great that some of the countries that had bailed out the banks started to go bust and had to be helped out themselves.

As a result, governments had to tax their people more, cut public services, and generally stop spending money wherever they could. Unemployment rose to horrific levels, particularly in southern Europe, and in some countries there were riots on the streets. As I write this letter, it seems that we have pulled out of this recession, but not without lots of pain, and lost jobs, homes and dreams.

But, of course, sometimes the pain is much deeper

than even the loss of a house or a job. The press reported the case of a man who took his life when the pressure of the £70,000 he owed on credit cards simply got too much for him. His widow described him as a 'vibrant, popular man who was such a lovely person'. Her husband had never spoken about the debts that had accumulated over three years and she said, 'I didn't know the full extent of the debt until two weeks after the death.'*

Such incidents often give rise to two questions. First: 'How could people have been so foolish as to take on loans they could not afford to repay?' The most hard-hearted commentators point out that people are responsible for their own actions – after all, banks don't *force* them to borrow money.

But the second question is: 'Why do banks lend money to people who manifestly can't afford to borrow it?' The answer from the banks is always along the same lines: 'It's not in our interest to give loans to people who can't repay them, and we have very stringent procedures to ensure we give good advice to our customers.' And yet, despite the banks' denials, in recent years so many people have had a different experience: the bank they used to trust implicitly now constantly tries to sell them things – and it's hard to say no.

* *The Daily Telegraph*, 12 March 2004.

Let me tell you why I have written to you about this. There may be a time in your life when you need to borrow money. You would have every right to think that you could trust the advice of those who are lending it to you, but you can't. Banks have short memories, and although they are being careful right now, all that will change with the sniff of an economic boom; then they'll be lending freely again. If you do need to borrow money – and most of us will at some time or other – then don't borrow more than you can afford to repay. Banks are great at giving you an umbrella when the sun is out; just don't expect to be able to hang on to it if it starts raining.

Be careful, and remember: lots of people have got into trouble because a bank manager said no, but millions more have done so because a bank manager said . . . yes.

12

Difficult people

IWONDER IF YOU would allow me to say a word or two about a challenge that you will have to deal with throughout your life: difficult people.

Now, if you are still relatively young when you read this, I can imagine what you might be thinking. It goes something like this: 'I have spent the best part of fifteen years of my life in school. I have come across plenty of difficult people – you should have met some of my teachers.' But if you think your maths teacher was truculent, made unreasonable demands on you, was downright grouchy and, in short, the most difficult person on the face of the planet, that is only because you haven't had more than one boss yet. You may not have met him or her, but somewhere down the road of your working life there is a manager who will make that old maths teacher seem like Father Christmas. In fact, exit interviews show that most people don't leave jobs – *they leave supervisors.*

But it's not just bosses. Whether you work in an office, on a building site, or get a job with NASA and spend your life orbiting the earth in a three-person space capsule, you will come across difficult people. So for what it's worth, here are some tips for dealing with these creatures.

The first is to realise that they will always be with you. When the railways began in the nineteenth century, the companies that ran them were experiencing an unacceptable level of accidents. One bright young engineer noticed that it was often the last carriage of the train that was involved in accidents and had a brilliant suggestion: they should *remove it*! The story doesn't say how long he held onto his job. Difficult people in our lives are like the last carriage on the train. We dream of the day they will be gone. We imagine them getting promotion to the Sydney office or sky-diving without a parachute, and daydream about what life will be like when they are gone. And then the day comes – our prayers have been answered! But does their leaving usher in an era of sweetness and light for us? No – before we know it, others rise up to take their place. In fact, the person who was reasonable, friendly, and one of our closest allies up until our difficult person left, now dons the 'difficult' mantle, and over the coming months and years makes you yearn for the Sydney office to send the last one back.

Difficult people will always be with us, so it is worth trying to live with them – after all, perhaps we are *their* difficult person and if we can change, they may too. But it is very important to realise that this is not always possible.

For many years I ran seminars for young lawyers who were at the start of their careers. I had many fascinating conversations at the end of those sessions, and one comes to my mind now. At first sight, the young solicitor who came to speak to me seemed self-assured and confident, but as she began to tell me her story, her head bowed and she started to cry. I asked her to tell me what troubled her. She said, 'My boss drags me down all the time. He finds fault with everything – the way I dress, my telephone manner . . . If I draft a document for him, he always finds *something* wrong with it, no matter how small.' She went on to say that she used to love work, but now she dreaded it. 'I am sick every morning before I go to the office, and my self-esteem is shattered. Sometimes I dig out my CV, gaze at the record of what I achieved in the past and think, "Where did that woman go? How did I move from being that self-assured person to the wreck I am today?"'

My advice to her was brief. 'Leave that office as soon as possible. This is not an issue with you; it is an issue with your boss. Unfortunately, you have a person managing you who is desperately insecure, and the way he deals with that is by putting other people down. When people *always* criticise, they reveal a deep flaw not in others, but in themselves, and you will *never* please them.'

She whispered, 'Thank you,' and brushed away a tear, but as she walked away, I sensed she held her head higher.

But how do we tell whether somebody who criticises us is really being helpful or not? The answer is to ask ourselves a question: 'Is this critic in the building business, or the demolition game?' The skills needed for both are, as you will know, quite different. For the one, you patiently lay a foundation and then carefully lay brick upon brick until something rises from the ground that you can be proud of. For the other, you go to something that another person has built and knock it down with a big steel ball.

Our critics are either builders or destroyers. Those who are builders have a single aim: they want to see us grow – to get better at what we do. The things they say to us are with the sole purpose of helping us develop. They are on our side, part of our team – if we were in a race, they would be shouting encouragement from the sidelines. At times, what they say to us may hurt (the book of Proverbs says, 'Faithful are the wounds of a friend'*), but they are on our side; they are *for* us.

Those in the second category are quite different. Their aim is not to build us up, but to bring us down. There may be no end to the opinions they will have about us and about what we are doing. They will comment on the way we dress, speak and style our hair. They will conduct personal appraisals of our work skills, our private life, the kind of car we drive, and how our children behave. But whatever it is they are critiquing, their aim is not to help us but to rob us of joy and peace in what we do.

You will never please these people.

Let me say that last sentence again, so that you really take it in, for unless you do, you could spend your whole life changing this and changing that, yet as soon as you do, your critics will simply move on to something else.

You will *never* please them!

But here's the tricky part about dealing with critics who are destroyers. Sometimes, even though they criticise you for the wrong reasons, there may still be a grain of truth in what they say. So, in a quiet moment, ponder and decide – for yourself – whether any of it is of value. But whether or not you want to make any changes, don't spend your life looking over your shoulder and wondering what

* Proverbs 27:6 KJV.

others are making of it. Some years ago a woman wrote saying, 'I have spent fifty years – half a century – imprisoned in other people's opinions of my life.'

Don't do time in that prison.

There is no freedom like knowing you have nothing to prove.

13

Bring me sunshine

ONE OF THE things I love so much about all you grandchildren at the ages you are right now is your irrepressible giggles; your smiles lighten up my life. And we laugh a lot together. I hope that you still laugh a lot by the time you read this. Sometimes, as you leave our house and your mother or father straps you into your car seat, I ask you, 'Shall Pops do something silly as you drive away?' You never say no. As soon as the car doors are closed, I duck down under your window and then crawl off and hide under a bush or behind the wheelie bins outside, and as your car goes by I leap out and jump about. You always laugh uncontrollably, although I have to admit that now, as I write about it, it doesn't seem all that hilarious. Perhaps both you and I need to get out a little more.

But I suppose that's just it: laughter in the family doesn't have to be complicated – in fact, sometimes the sillier the better. The other day one of you was looking through the books that I have written and said, 'Pops, are you famous?' Well, I once got recognised by somebody in a service station on the M6 motorway and they asked me to sign a book but, to be honest, that's about it. In fact, it's the kind of famous where nobody has heard of you. But if I have any tiny bit of fame, then it's to do with something silly. In one of my first books, *The Sixty Minute Father* (you girls mustn't even think of marrying a man who can't recite large chunks of it back to you), I wrote about the fun we used to have with your parents when they were small.

We used to call it 'Family Night'. Once a week your parents would drag their mattresses into Nandi's and my bedroom, and sleep on the floor. But once a month we used to have a 'Super Family Night'. This was quite an occasion. On a Saturday night we would all drag our mattresses downstairs, and sleep on the living room floor. The fire would be lit, and we would listen to story tapes in the dark and eat chocolate. (A woman once berated me for allowing my children to eat chocolate late at night – she told me their teeth would rot. I'd like to send her a photograph of your parents' gnashers now and tell her to get a life, but that wouldn't be nice!)

For some reason, that little book sold throughout the world in twenty languages, and all over the globe people started to have family nights. I am responsible for more strained backs caused by dragging mattresses downstairs than I care to think about. Sometimes people write to me to tell me their own experiences of these occasions. Here's a recent email from a man who did just that.

We think, sure, always up to try something for our family — let's 'do a Rob Parsons'.

Stage 1: drag mattresses down from bedrooms.

Problem: my wife and I can't lift our mattress; it is king size and two grown men struggle to move it.

Solution: my wife and daughter can share the bed settee, we will get our son's mattress down, and I will sleep on an air mattress in a sleeping bag.

Bed: check, movie: check, sweets: check, chocolate and fizzy pop: check.

All OK so far.

Watch movie, eat all the sweets and chocolate, drink the fizzy pop — all going really well. Thank you, Rob Parsons, for such a good family idea.

Movie ends. Four-year-old daughter ricochets round the room like a bullet in sugar-fuelled rush and excitement that we are all sleeping in the same room together.

Rest of the family tries to get to sleep.

Finally get to sleep.

Frighten the children with my snoring.

Wake up and find my wife and children upstairs in my bed. No room for me. Try to sleep in sleeping bag on the floor. Fail.

Next day: entire family sleep-deprived; four-year-old daughter in particularly foul mood.

Thank you for a good memory and keep up the brilliant work you do. We now have a giggle when we remember the night we 'did a Rob Parsons'.

Darren

Did you spot the magic word in Darren's letter – the word that makes all the trauma of that night worth it? It was in the last sentence: *Remember.*

What Darren and his family did that night was to make a memory. It doesn't matter how you do it, but whether it's with friends or family, make sure you create those memories. They rarely cost much money, and they are sweeter if at least part of the memory is helpless laughter.

As I look back over our family life – back when your parents were kids – there is one story that, for me, sums all this up. I have told it all over the world. Sometimes people ask me, 'Is it really true?' I am afraid it is – every word.

We were on a family holiday and near where we were

staying there was a big lake where people were fishing. Suddenly Lloyd said, 'Dad, can we go fishing?'

I replied, 'We haven't got a rod, son,' but he was fourteen and he was not to be stopped.

He found a long twig and tied a piece of string on to make a line. He put a safety pin on to act as a hook and attached a big lump of bread from one of his sandwiches to the end of it. Never in the history of the world have fish been in so little danger. They examined the bread, picked bits off at will, and shared it out among their friends and neighbours.

Despite this, I was getting quite engrossed in our little effort – and that's when it happened: I suddenly heard a loud noise from further along the bank. I turned and saw a group of fishermen. They had expensive rods and every conceivable fishing aid . . . and they were laughing at us. Now, I'm not proud of what happened next, but I threw our makeshift rod to the floor and stalked off across the road. I made my way to a restaurant, where I had earlier seen some dead fish displayed outside for sale. I bought one; it cost me almost five pounds.

I rushed back to the lake and, as surreptitiously as possible, secured the fish to the safety pin on the end of our rod and lowered the line into the lake. I said, 'Lloyd, when some people come past, I want you to yell out as loud as you can, "Dad, I think you've got one!"'

He gave me a sympathetic look, but said, 'OK, I'll do it.'

After about five minutes, a group of people came towards us along the little path that skirted the lake. When they drew near he yelled out, 'Dad, I think you've got one!' The people turned to look and, to my delight, so did the fishermen who had been laughing at us. I pulled on the twig and yanked the string from the water. The fish was firmly fixed to the end, its scales glinting in the afternoon sun – a fine specimen indeed.

I turned to the crowd to enjoy my moment, but instead of looks of admiration, there were signs of acute embarrassment. People started talking among themselves and sidled off along the path. The fishermen further along were sniggering. I didn't understand. 'What went wrong, Lloyd?'

He was helpless with laughter. In fact, he was rolling on the grass, holding his sides. It took several minutes before he could say anything, but finally he spluttered it out: 'Two things, Dad. First, you should have jiggled the line a bit – the fish looked *so* dead!' And then he paused and started laughing again. 'And second, you put the hook . . . through its *tail*.'

I promise you that as a parent I have tried my very best to pass on values to my kids: to let them know what I believe is important in life, and to teach them right from wrong. But I think that we would all have missed something special if, when I was gone, they didn't say, 'The old boy was crazy sometimes, wasn't he? Do you remember the things he had us doing?'

Going back to *The Sixty Minute Father* book that I mentioned a few moments ago, this is how I ended one of the chapters:

Fun rarely has to have a large price ticket attached to it. Fun is borrowing a tent and sleeping in the garden. It's going to the cinema on a school night once a year, and it's having water fights. It's saying in traffic, 'The next car we pass will be driven by the kind of man that Gemma will marry', pulling up to the car opposite, gazing into it and hearing the children falling about helplessly while you try to keep a little composure.

I admit there could be dangers with all of those examples. You could get pneumonia in the garden, and we know it's not good to stay up late on school nights. The water could hit an electricity cable and send the whole neighbourhood up in flames. And the man in the car could be an axe-murderer who takes your car number. But it will probably be OK . . . and you will laugh with your children.

The day will surely come when you will cry with

them. They may be thirteen or thirty and you will have your arms around each other as you go through a tough family time together. No home is immune from such experiences. But home life needs to be a tapestry of tough times and moments of helpless laughter.

When they were very young, you used to tickle them.

Don't ever stop.

14

Slaying your dragons

T HERE ARE FOUR basic emotions: anger, fear, happiness and sadness. I wonder which of them affects us most. I think that for many of us it is fear. The strange thing is that so often it's hard to put our finger on what we are actually afraid of; it's simply that somewhere deep inside us there is an ever-present gnawing anxiety. I remember reading your parents the *Mr Men* series of books when they were small. One of the characters was called Mr Worry. This dear man was plagued by fear. He would worry about his car, his dog, his house and his dinner. And when he had nothing to worry about, he got even more concerned, for he was sure he had missed something important to worry about, and that bothered him more than anything. His thoughts would race and cause him to imagine all sorts of problems that could occur. And, so often, those runaway thoughts led him into fear.

I sympathise with Mr Worry. I remember once lying in bed in the morning and imagining a conversation with somebody. In my mind this person said something that annoyed me. I replied angrily. They shot back a stunning insult, and I delivered a withering riposte. And then my thoughts really began to run away with me. I started to worry about it all. But just as a headache was beginning to form over my right eye, I realised that the whole thing had only occurred in my mind. No one had said anything nasty to me at all. I had not *actually* had a row with any-body. In fact, there was no real problem – and it was probably time to get out of bed.

That's only one of hundreds of times I've had those runaway thoughts that lead to fear. I've had them about examinations, money, jobs and friends, to name just a few subjects. Oh, and my health. Before the wonders of the Internet, we used to have something at home called *The Doctor's Book*, which allowed you to look up the symptoms of various ailments. The only problem was that every time I consulted the thing, I became instantly convinced I not only had the illness I had looked up, but the one on the facing page as well.

And I've had runaway thoughts when your parents were teenagers and they were a little late coming in at night

– especially Lloyd. About ten minutes after his curfew I would smile nervously at your grandmother and start to make tea, saying, 'He'll be in soon.' And then, just as I was filling up the kettle, my thoughts would race off and within moments I would be full of fear. I would imagine police cars pulling up at our door, hospitals ringing us with news of accidents, or him ringing us from Gretna Green saying, 'We've tied the knot. Do you want to chip in some money for the honeymoon?'

We have probably all experienced that kind of runaway fear at one time or another, but I have met people who live their whole lives defined by their fears. They are afraid of failure, and they are even afraid of success, for if they succeed somebody may ask them to repeat the trick. Of course, fear is a healthy emotion; it is a part of our design, and keeps us safe – if a predator is nearby then fear is a very useful emotion to have. But when fear takes us over, it can paralyse us. And so often these fears are totally unfounded. Mark Twain said, 'Most of my tragedies have never happened to me.'

Early mapmakers used to draw mythical beasts or sea monsters to designate areas that remained unknown; along the edge of one old map is a warning not to venture further, with the words: 'Here be dragons.' These explorers had never seen a dragon, and dragons never were found in any of the new places they discovered, but beyond the charted edges of the map was the future – and the future was always unknown. Often, when these new territories were eventually explored, they were discovered to be places of wonderful beauty, rich resources and staggering opportunity. But until that time, these undiscovered lands were represented by those fearful words and symbols.

Sometimes we put limits on how we live our lives with those words: 'Here be dragons.' But if we stay within the confines we've set, while we may be safe from harm, and perhaps even from emotional hurt, there will be new worlds of experience and achievement that we will never discover.

When I was in the Middle East some years ago, I spent a few minutes watching a camel owner who was giving rides to tourists. Giggling teenagers bounced along, ageing bodies held grimly onto the reins and, to the delight of the watching crowd, one super-cool thirty-something went flying over the beast's head! But my main memory is of a small boy. He could have been no more than five years old. A little earlier his father had led him and his older sister to see the camel at close quarters. The animal towered above them, occasionally showing teeth that made the wolf in Red Riding Hood look positively gummy. The worldly wise sibling, who was all of ten, confidently stroked the camel, while her brother poked a hand out nervously towards it from behind his father's back.

But now it was the big moment, and he and his sister had the chance to ride. The boy watched wide-eyed as his sister was lifted onto the camel. As she began her short journey he ran from behind his father's back and waved at her, laughing loudly. He was totally captivated, enjoying every moment. But then, as the camel turned to come back, I could see his small face change as an awful reality dawned on him: it was his turn next.

He ran straight back behind his father, and no amount of cajoling from either father or camel owner would get him anywhere near the animal. Finally the dad gave up, paid for his daughter's ride, took both children's hands and started off down the street. They had gone about ten metres when I saw something that moved me greatly: the small boy stopped, turned, looked wistfully back at the camel and then continued down the road. That look conveyed what he couldn't say in words: 'I desperately want to try . . . but I just can't.'

I have seen that look so often – in the eyes not of children, but of adults. It conveys something that I have sometimes felt in my own spirit. It is a look that gazes at opportunity, that caresses a dream, or that imagines a relationship, but is paralysed – paralysed by fear.

There is an incredible poster of Taylor Knox, one of the world's greatest surfers, that shows him in front of a huge wave (over fifty feet high!) at Todos Santos in

Mexico. Underneath are the words, 'What if your fears and dreams existed in the same place?'

By nature I can be a fearful person and allow the fear of failure to hold me back – perhaps stop me from trying something new – but sometimes we have to have the courage to press on.

The story goes that a finance officer of a large company who specialised in pouring cold water on the CEO's every dream said to his boss one day: 'But what if your new idea doesn't work?'

The CEO shrugged his shoulders. 'No problem,' he replied. 'If it doesn't, we'll just go back to doing what wasn't working before.'

I like what President Theodore Roosevelt said:

> It is not the critic who counts . . . The credit belongs to the man who is actually in the arena, whose face is marred by dust and sweat and blood; . . . who at the best knows in the end the triumph of high achievement, and who at the worst, if he fails, at least fails while daring greatly, so that his place shall never be with those cold and timid souls who know neither victory nor defeat.*

* Excerpt from a speech by Theodore Roosevelt, 'Citizenship in a Republic', delivered at the Sorbonne, in Paris, France on 23 April 1910.

As I think of these things, I imagine a small boy suddenly stopping in a dusty street and turning to yell at an old man leading a camel: 'Hey, mister! I've changed my mind!'

15

'Saving' time

ONE OF THE lessons we looked at previously was about regrets that people express at the end of their lives: 'I wish I'd had the courage to live a life true to myself, not the life others expected of me.' Another one is this: 'I wish I hadn't worked so hard.' I can honestly tell you, I've heard that said countless times, mainly by men not at the end of their lives, but in their fifties and sixties.

But actually, I don't believe 'I wish I hadn't worked so hard' is the *real* regret. Most people I have spoken to about this issue don't regret working too hard, they really regret spending *too much time* working. There's a well-known saying that sums this up succinctly: 'Nobody ever said on their death-bed, "I wish I'd spent more time at the office."'

Many of these people told me that working long hours, either in the office or stuck in front of the computer at home, just became a lifestyle. One man said that he believes he could have achieved just as much if he'd worked fewer hours, but he simply became addicted to work. Of course, many men and women have to work long hours or do several jobs just to make ends meet, but that's a different thing to *choosing* to live that way. And the truth is that this problem does not apply just to paid work; we all have the capacity to fill our time so that we are endlessly busy. If we are a bit insecure, this busyness can often help us to feel valuable in the eyes of others, but it is a dreadful trap.

Many of us don't wake up to this fact until it's too late, because we have never grasped that irrespective of our age, intellect and income, we are all affected by the same limitation: *time.* Every man, woman and child has the same amount at their disposal – one thousand four hundred and forty minutes a day. You have exactly the same allocation, whether you are the president of the United States or the person who cleans the White House toilets.

And the fact that time is limited means that every choice as to how we spend it precludes some other possibility. If you're working at your desk at 7.30 in the evening, you can't be reading your son a bedtime story. When your parents were young, I made some bad mistakes in this area. I, too, confused working hard with working *long*. Putting in those extra hours helped me convince myself I was successful. The fact that I could often have done the work in less time and gone home an hour earlier was beside the point.

It may be that when we last spoke I couldn't string three sentences together, so this could be hard for you to believe, but I have had the privilege of speaking to over a million people throughout the world. Many are very successful in their chosen professions, but one thing I often urge them not to forget is the fact that although work is important, when they are older it is in the area of relationships that they will judge their success. I warn them that if they have children, those kids will be grown and gone before they know it. As I speak, there are the usual looks of disbelief from the young, and knowing nods from those with a few grey hairs. I say, 'The days when your children want you to watch them in school plays, teach them to fly a kite, and listen to that story over and over again are very limited. The time is hurtling towards you when you're going to say to a fifteen-year-old, "Do you fancy going bowling on Saturday?" and he'll reply, "Do you mind if we don't, Dad? I said I'd go out with some friends."'

The other day I had dinner with a man who is at the very top of his profession in the computer world. He told me that researchers are discovering that many people are now addicted to technology – mobile phones, iPods, computers. I must admit, that wasn't a surprise to me. Recently I heard a man talk about an incident that occurred with his young son. He said:

> It was about 7 p.m. and since I'd got home from work half an hour earlier, I'd been doing my email. Every few minutes my son had been trying to get my attention, but I'd carried on with the email. Ethan came up to me yet again and grabbed my arm: 'Dad, can I show you something I painted in school today?' I snapped back at him, 'Can't you see I'm busy?' His head dropped and as he walked away I heard my seven-year-old comment: 'You're a nicer person without your iPhone.'

Getting the balance right is never easy, but one day I did a little maths that changed my life. I worked out the number of days in the first eighteen years of my children's lives – six thousand five hundred and seventy. No amount of success, money or prestige can buy you one day more. If your child is ten years old, you have two thousand nine hundred and twenty left. I understand as well as anybody the pressures of modern life, but those days of your children's lives are irreplaceable: so far as is possible, try not to miss one of them. When I was speaking in Cape Town once, a man came up to me at the end of my presentation. He was a multimillionaire – and he was crying. He said, 'Where were you twenty years ago when my family was young?'

What is it that lures so many of us into a life of busyness in which we manage to find time for almost everything except those we love the most? I think that maybe it's the belief that there will always be tomorrow – when life will be slower. We tell ourselves that in the future we'll have lots of time for those we care about. And that would be true if only we could 'save' time – to somehow 'carry it forward' – but we can't.

I've mentioned Steve Jobs, the founder of Apple, before. He has been called 'the greatest inventor since Edison'. He died in 2011. In one obituary the writer said that the devices Jobs created 'saved time' for billions of people around the world, as documents, music and ideas could now be transmitted in nanoseconds. But the obituary writer was wrong: Jobs's inventions certainly allowed people to do those tasks faster, but they didn't *save* time. You can't save time – you can only *spend* it. People say, 'I saved an hour.' Really? Then where is that hour now? Hidden under the bed? Stashed away in a safe for the day when you are so very busy that you will need it? No. Even as you 'saved' it, you spent it on something else.

And that's the regret that hits so many of us in later life. We have spent all our time in giving everything to our job, but now we are sixty and the job has just given us a clock with our name on it (ironic that it's so often a clock!). Suddenly we have lots of time spare, but what we crave now are good relationships . . . however, so often it's too late.

Brian Dyson, CEO of Coca-Cola Enterprises, described this dilemma by imagining life as a game in which we are juggling five balls: work, family, health, friends and spirit. We go through life trying to keep all of these in the air. At first we give all the balls the same priority, but one day we discover that they are not all the same. The work ball is made of rubber: if you drop it, it will (normally) bounce back. But the other four balls — family, health, friends and spirit — are made of glass. If you drop one of these they are easily damaged or may even shatter. Taking a little extra care with these balls is a wise decision.

I hope you are already doing, or will be able to find, a job that you love. And I hope you give that job your very best shot. But don't give your soul to it, and don't let anybody ever try to convince you that a slower day is coming.

16

Forgiveness

A T THE HEART of what has come to be known as the Lord's Prayer are thirteen words: 'And forgive us our trespasses as we forgive those who trespass against us.'* The thirteen words are always said together, yet in truth the two halves of the sentence are quite different. The first five roll off our tongues easily. We know that if there is a God in heaven then we are going to need his forgiveness day in, day out, for both the small things and the great. The last eight words, though, are often voiced without real consideration of the consequences. It is not that we are insincere; we understand that if we receive forgiveness from God, then the least we can do is to offer

* *The Book of Common Prayer*, 1662.

it to our fellow human beings. No, the problem is not whether we mean the words we say, it is our failure to act on them when the promise is called in.

Alexander Pope said, 'To err is human, to forgive is divine.' And if anybody hurts you – really hurts you – you will discover why people have come to believe that forgiveness is truly a supernatural act. On a human level one could understand that if we are to survive as a species, revenge would be a much better option than forgiveness. If somebody knew that there would be fast and furious retribution when they hurt you, obviously it would be a genuine disincentive.

And it's that philosophy that largely governs how many of us live our lives. If somebody quickly slips into a parking space for which we have been waiting patiently, our first thought is not forgiveness. Whether or not they took our space knowingly, we treat them the same: we sound our horn, we gesticulate, and if they are very small or very old, we may feel brave enough to actually get out of our car and remonstrate with them. As we are making rude signs and threatening all manner of sanctions, if somebody suggested to us that we should consider forgiveness, then our argument would go something like this: 'That's all very well, but you can't go through life letting people walk all over you.' That reply seems so sensible that it practically finishes the argument. The only problem is that if it works for a stolen parking place, then what hope have we got in trying to forgive a deep hurt delivered at the hands of a work colleague, an unjust sacking by a boss, a betrayal by a friend, or an ungrateful child who breaks our heart?

But the problem is not just that we don't believe life will work if we forgive too freely. Sometimes it just seems plain wrong to forgive. We may hear somebody like Gordon Wilson from Northern Ireland, whose daughter died in his arms, saying that he forgave the terrorists who killed her, but we feel they have no right to be forgiven. And in that conclusion we are correct – none of us has a *right* to be forgiven. So is there something else going on here?

Well, perhaps we should first establish what forgiveness is not. It is not saying, 'What you did didn't hurt me deeply.' It is not saying, 'I can forgive and forget' – how can we possibly forget a deep hurt? It is not saying, 'You should not face the normal sanctions of the law or any other tribunal for what you have done.' And if we believe in God, then it is not saying that those who do wrong will not have to answer to him one day. One of the most poignant newspaper cartoons of the last world war was set in a concentration camp. A line of Jewish people are being mown down by a stormtrooper with a machine gun. We know that the Nazis were meticulous in keeping records – even of their atrocities – and behind the stormtrooper is an officer who has a notebook and pencil, noting the date and names of the victims. But as he fires, the gunner is only partly looking at those he is killing – his face is half turned and he is gazing at a figure in white who is standing behind the colonel. It is apparent that the officer cannot see the angel at all, but in the angel's hand is a notebook and in it he too is making a record of names and dates.

But if we have established, at least in part, what forgiveness is not, then what is it? Well, of course, forgiveness is multi-layered, but let me dwell for a moment on just one of those layers. What if the act of forgiveness is partly selfish? Now I don't mean 'selfish' in the normal, negative sense, but in the sense that forgiving is better for *us*. In other words, could it be true that those who are able to forgive – who stop nursing the wrong, who avoid the sheer pleasure of hearing the stories of others who have been hurt by the person who hurt us, who refuse to believe that the perpetrator could never change, and who decide to move on with their lives – *do better*. The old Chinese proverb suggests that those who cannot forgive and continue to harbour revenge must dig *two* graves. We pursue the one who has hurt us, we make them pay in every way for what they have done to us – in essence we 'bury' them. But the bitterness, the anger, and perhaps even the sheer frustration of the feeling that even then they deserve worse – eventually 'kills' us also.

And sometimes the wrong that has been done to us so permeates our thoughts – and every other area of our lives – that it comes to define us. It is all we talk about. It becomes the reason we give for every minor and major problem or dissatisfaction in our life. We practically clutch it to our chest; we cannot live without it.

Black Angel,* a play by Michael Christofer, tells the story of Herman Engel, a military general who was sentenced to thirty years' imprisonment for crimes against humanity. After he has completed his sentence he decides to hide away from those he knows would still like to exact the ultimate punishment. At the time of the play he is in Alsace with his wife and they are building a cabin deep in the woods.

But what Engel does not know is that he was followed to the cabin by a journalist called Morrieu whose entire family and village were killed by Engel's soldiers. For thirty years Morrieu has lived for the day when he could himself carry out the sentence on Engel that he believes the court should have passed. He goes to a nearby village and whips up hatred in the hearts of the people towards their new neighbour. The villagers

---

* Michael Christofer, *Black Angel*, Dramatists Play Service, June 1986.

decide that when darkness falls they will go into the wood and kill Engel.

But Morrieu first wants to talk with the person whose death he has desired for so long – he has so many unanswered questions. He goes to the cabin and suddenly he is face to face with the man he has hated for thirty years. But instead of the monster he had anticipated meeting, there is a frail old man and, worse, as Engel begins to tell his side of the story, Morrieu's desire for revenge fades and he begins to doubt his course of action.

Finally Morrieu can stand it no longer. He blurts out, 'The villagers are coming to kill you tonight.' He offers to lead Engel out of the wood and save him. And then an incredible thing happens. Engel says, 'I'll go with you on one condition: *that you forgive me.*'

Morrieu cannot deal with this. He has hated this man for over a quarter of a century; he has lain awake at night planning his revenge. But now he is unsure what to do. And then he decides. He is willing to save the man's life, but he cannot forgive him. True to his word, Engel stays in the cabin and that night he dies at the hands of the villagers.

The play urges us to consider a single question: why was it harder for Morrieu to forgive his enemy than to save his life? Commenting on the play, Professor Lewis Smedes puts it like this: 'It was too much for Morrieu [to forgive], because hatred had become a passion too long lodged in his soul. He could not live, could no longer be the person he was, without his hatred; he had *become* his hatred. His hatred did not belong to him, he *belonged* to his hate. He would not know who he was if he did not hate Engel.'*

In the work I have done, I have met many men and women who had to grapple with the issue of forgiveness. It is never easy – none of us should ever make it seem so. But it is also true that I have often had the privilege of observing the transformational power of forgiveness. I have never forgotten this letter I received from a woman who had attended a marriage seminar almost twenty-five years ago:

Dear Rob,

On Saturday my husband and I attended the *Marriage Matters* seminar. It was a day that changed our lives. In the morning, before leaving our home, I said to my husband, 'I think this seminar is our last hope; if nothing good comes of this day, I think we may have to part.' You see after fourteen years of marriage, he had an affair. I've

---

* Lewis Smedes, *How Can It Be All Right When Everything is All Wrong* (Authentic, 2011).

not been able to forgive him. However sorry he said he was, I simply could not. That was until Saturday. But when you spoke about the possibility of forgiveness . . . I thought, how can I not forgive? And your words made me think so much about my children, my little girl and my little boy; they deserve a happy life, a mother and a father to love and to care for them. The whole day made us look at our family, and we talked so much that night, and we're still talking. We laughed a lot and at the end of the day we cried together. Thank you. Saturday changed our lives . . .

I have thought often about that woman. I know that forgiveness like that is not always possible, but *she* decided to give it.

Forgiveness is not magic. When we try to forgive it does not mean that the memories or the hurts will go, that we won't occasionally still wake with that sick feeling in our stomachs, or that we won't still have to look away when we pass a place that brings back painful recollections. But for that couple, forgiveness gave them a chance: it was the key that allowed them to try again, at least. In fact, ten years after her first letter, the woman sent me a photograph. It was of her, her husband, and their two teenage children smiling out at the camera. I turned the Polaroid over and over in my hand and wondered at the story that lay behind it, and whether the children knew, or would ever know, about what had nearly torn their home apart. And I thought of a woman's resolve and the sheer courage it often takes to even begin *to forgive*.

17
The spider's web

WHEN I WAS a child my mother used to quote two sayings to me pretty regularly. The first was 'Be sure your sin will find you out.' Now I must admit that for much of my young life I believed this to be completely true. She used to have an uncanny ability to suss out any misdemeanour in which I had engaged. There was no CCTV then – it was the 1950s, for goodness' sake – but, honestly, it was as if my mother had cameras everywhere and monitored them from her kitchen.

As I got older I realised that, at least in this life, the saying is not always true. There were loads of things I did in my teenage years that she never discovered – thankfully. Having said that, the American sociologist Dr Tony Campolo says that when he was a kid, the leaders in his church used to tell him that after you die you stand before God and he shows a video of your whole life to everybody – *and your mother will be there*! I certainly hope not. If she sees me aged fifteen snogging Rita Allsop and smoking at the same time, heaven itself will not be big enough for me to get away from her wrath.

My mother's second saying is actually a quote from a poem by Sir Walter Scott: 'Oh, what a tangled web we weave, when first we practise to deceive.' The first lie is often innocuous and seemingly harmless – perhaps even what we would call a 'white lie'; but the second leads us, lie by further lie, into a web which eventually entraps us completely. Allow me to tell you a true story.

Marcus Einfeld was one of the most distinguished judges in Australia, a Queen's Counsel who sat in the Supreme Court. But it was not only within his professional calling that he was honoured. He was declared Australian National Treasure in 1997 and was given the United Nations Peace Award in 2002. There was a good reason for all this honour. Einfeld had been the founding President of the Australian Human Rights and Equal Opportunities Commission. In 1987 he headed a major investigation into the living conditions of Aborigines and famously shed tears when he heard evidence during the hearing that a young boy who had been denied a proper rugby ball had played instead with an old shoe. It was fair to say that at the age of seventy, Einfeld was distinguished, wealthy and at the top of his profession.

Everything changed on 8 January 2008. It was a Tuesday afternoon, at one minute past four. Einfield was driving his silver-grey Lexus when he went through a speed camera at six miles per hour above the limit of thirty. Ten days later he received in the post a speeding ticket, a fine of $77 (about £36) and was notified that his driving licence would be debited with three penalty points.

Einfeld turned the speeding ticket over and over in his hands. The problem wasn't the £36 fine – it was that he already had some penalty points and three further points would bring him closer to losing his licence. If he had thought about that for just a moment he would have realised that although an embarrassment, it was not terminal, and although an inconvenience, it was not insurmountable: he could afford to hire a chauffeur for six months. But Einfeld decided on a different course of action. He lied.

He told the court that, actually, on the day in question he had lent his car to an old friend, Professor Teresa Brennan, an American academic who was now back in the United States. The court accepted his story without question and the speeding ticket was nullified.

You may remember that I said a little earlier that my mother's first saying didn't always come true (at least in this life), but on this occasion it did – Einfield was about to be found out. Sitting in court that day was a young reporter, Viva Goldner. She took what appeared to be a routine story back to her paper, a Sydney tabloid called the *Daily Telegraph*, where it was destined to get a few column inches on an inside page. But a seasoned reporter on the paper, Michael Beach, thought he would do a quick Google search to check the spelling of Teresa Brennan's name. He discovered that she had been killed in a hit-and-run accident three years before Einfield had been caught speeding.

Michael Beach told Viva Goldner to try to find a home phone number for the judge and ask him to clear up the mystery. The following is her recollection of that telephone call.

I just rang him and said we needed to double-check that it was Teresa Brennan who was driving the car, and he said it was, and I told him that we'd checked on the Internet and that the accident she was killed in happened before the speeding fine. He then went quiet and I asked him if he was there, and he said yes. So I asked him how it could be possible that she was driving his car if she was dead. And he paused and then said it was the other Teresa Brennan. I asked him if there were two of them, and he said yes. I asked if she was also from Florida as it said in his statutory declaration and he said, 'Yes, yes, I think so', and then he said he wasn't sure if it was Theresa with an 'h' or Therese, but that there were definitely two of them. He didn't know where she was now, and then he said, 'I have nothing more to say' and hung up.

Marcus Einfeld had begun to weave the tangled web that Walter Scott had written about, and now he thought he couldn't stop. He produced for the court a detailed twenty-page declaration concerning a second Teresa Brennan who, he said, also lived in the United States and whom he had met in Bangladesh. The declaration was vivid in detail about the scenes and the conversations they'd had – and totally fictitious.

In a news interview about the case he said, 'I categorically deny that I was the driver of my car on January 8th 2006 in Mosman. On January 8th I was out of Sydney ... I again unequivocally and categorically deny any suggestion of wrongdoing on my part.'

As the case went on, Einfeld said that he'd suddenly remembered that he had in fact been driving his mother's Toyota Corolla that day, so he couldn't have been at the wheel of his Lexus. His ninety-four-year-old mother duly signed a statement to that effect. Detectives began to scour hours of CCTV footage from his mother's apartment block. It showed that between daylight and dusk her car had not left its garage.

Einfeld eventually admitted his guilt. Supreme Court Justice Bruce James found Einfeld had committed 'deliberate, premeditated perjury' that was 'part of planned criminal activity'. He was sentenced to three years in prison with a non-parole period of two years for knowingly making a false statement under oath and for attempting to pervert the course of justice. The President of the New South Wales Bar Association successfully applied to the Court of Appeal to revoke Einfeld's commission as Queen's Counsel, on the basis that his conduct had brought shame upon the legal profession as well as on himself.

Einfeld's mother died, aged ninety-nine, almost as soon as he got out of jail. He said he felt as if she had been waiting for him. Perhaps the most tragic part of the whole affair was a brief conversation he had with her when he was trying to persuade her to say he had borrowed her car. 'Mum, remember how you lent me your Toyota that day?' he said, and she responded, 'Marcus, what have you got yourself into?' Suddenly he was a little boy again.

I tell you this story not because it is unusual; it is only unusual in the stature of the person in question – the height he had to fall. In fact, the act is repeated every day in schools, colleges, factories, offices and homes. Decent men and women decide to tell a simple lie to make life easier for the moment, not knowing that subsequent and deeper fictions will be required to bolster the shaky foundations of the first. Marcus Einfeld didn't lose everything; he still had the love of family and friends. But he did lose a lot – perhaps even his own sense of self-worth. When I first heard his story it seemed to me that Sir Walter Scott's image of the spider's web of deceit was an apt one. Never in a hundred years would Einfeld have decided in one go to tell all the lies that eventually came from his mouth and his pen. But to trap him, the spider didn't need him to: he just had to tell the first.

When we began talking about this particular lesson, I said that your great-grandmother had two sayings that she repeated time after time. Actually there were three. I suppose I hesitated to mention the third because it can seem so trite or patronising – even unrealistic – in a world where every issue is not clear cut. Nevertheless, I have decided I *will* tell you it in the hope that its sheer simplicity will perhaps one day save you (and perhaps the reminder of it will save me) from taking the first tragic step towards entrapment in that tangled web. I have no doubt that it would have saved Marcus Einfeld if he had taken a moment to consider its power:

'It's always right to do what's right.'

18

An attitude of gratitude

THE OTHER DAY, I asked your grandmother if she ever thought that I was selfish. I honestly thought she'd reply, 'You are one of the least selfish people I have ever known.' Instead, she sighed and said, 'You know what, Rob? Most of us are more selfish than we'd like to believe.'

I think she is right. The truth is, it's easy to be selfish. There's seems to be a part of our make-up that makes us think first: 'What is best for me?' And when that thought kicks in, it can cause us to become unbelievably upset at the slightest disturbance or inconvenience in our lives. I have just heard on the news that a sixty-year-old man has been imprisoned for killing another pensioner who stole his parking space at a supermarket.[*]

Of course, a by-product of this is that we can become so concerned with our own little world that we become impervious to the suffering of others – even if their hardship is so much greater than ours. A friend of mine calls these sorts of nagging worries (freezers breaking down, losing TV remote controls, filling cars with diesel instead of petrol) 'First World problems'. William Hazlitt put it well: 'The least pain in our little finger gives us more concern than the destruction of millions of our fellow human-beings.' But selfish people can never be happy for long, for the very simple reason that life is never perfect for long.

When I was a teenager, I went to a little church – the Gospel Hall – on the corner of my street. The church of my youth had lots of things going for it, but excitement wasn't one of them. And it was in search of a little excitement that my friend Carl and I used to occasionally desert our 'local' and sneak into the large Pentecostal church in the heart of our city. If the leaders from the Gospel Hall had caught us within fifty yards of the place we'd have been excommunicated at the very least, but the second

[*] http://news.sky.com/story/1181513/asda-car-park-row-death-pensioner-jailed [accessed 12 December 2013].

we walked through the doors of the City Temple, Carl and I knew it was worth the risk. We were wide-eyed. Whereas our little place of worship had pews, the Pentecostals had cinema seats. We had a hundred members, they had a thousand – which meant that the selection of girls was truly awesome. But I remember the singing most of all. In my church we sang as though it was a punishment and every note caused us pain, but these people sang as though they had been drinking. And what songs they were – so positive! My favourite was 'Count your blessings, name them one by one, and it will surprise you what the Lord has done'.

One day the pastor spoke about that song and told us it was wrong to take God for granted – that God liked us to be grateful. He told us to make sure that we thanked God every day for the good things he has given us. I loved singing that song, but adulthood robbed me of the joy in it. Cynicism picked at the words, sophistication complained about the melody, and the everyday hassles reminded me that life wasn't easy; pain was everywhere, and silly, shallow songs had no place in a mature man's repertoire of music.

I stopped singing that hymn. But we all have to sing a song of some sort and instead I chose one called, 'Count your problems, name them one by one'. And there has never been any shortage of things to count. I remember a particularly disastrous time when my central heating broke down, I lost my mobile phone and the washing machine leaked – all in the space of a week.

And then, when I was forty years old, I went to Africa. I saw shanty towns where tens of thousands of people live with no running water and no proper sewage system. Often there are families of six in a room ten feet by ten, with a few planks of wood for walls and a bit of tin for a roof. And some of them were hungry, and some of them had AIDS, and all of them would have given almost anything to live in a house where the central heating broke down once in while.

You must never let anybody convince you that men shouldn't cry. The problem with most of us is that we don't cry enough. I cried a lot on that Africa trip. I cried at the sight of thirteen-year-old girls lining up to sell their bodies. I cried at babies' cots being nibbled by rats. And I cried at kids with huge eyes and no hope.

Sometimes life ambushes us and, when it does, it is always painful. But once in a while, the experience brings some good with it. I got ambushed in Africa, and I vowed then with all my heart that I was going to try to appreciate the good things – including the people – I have in my life. And I was going to try to get less screwed up about what doesn't really matter. I was going to at least attempt to develop what somebody once called 'an attitude of gratitude'. I was moved by something said by an older person looking back over the years: 'What a wonderful life I've had. I only wish I'd realised it sooner.'*

I decided to start singing the old song again.

* Sidonie G. Collette.

19

The eighth wonder of the world

WE'VE SPOKEN ALREADY about being in debt. People who have never known the gut-wrenching worry of financial trauma will never understand why sometimes it just seems easier to stick the bills in the cupboard and hope the whole sorry mess goes away. But debt never just goes away; unless we deal with it, it always gets worse. And, like so many of the ogres we meet in life, when we face this particular one head on, it often turns out not to be as frightening as we first thought. A while ago, I wrote a book about it, called *The Money Secret*. It's in the form of a novel, and I'm sure you know what you must never do with novels – skip straight to the last page to see how it all ends. But in this case, because I'm not at all certain that by the time you're an adult you'll be able to find a copy of my book, let alone read it, let me take you straight to the very last page and tell you 'the money secret' now. It's this: *spend less than you earn.*

Those last five words seem so simple, don't they? In fact, I bet you hardly noticed them. But listen again: *spend less than you earn.* Until you grasp this, you will be tied to debt and debt will be tied to you as surely as if you were in chains together. You may think that the answer to debt is to earn more: well, in some cases, you're right; some people are just too poor. They don't need ten tips on budgeting; they need more money. But for the vast majority of people, getting out of debt has very little to do with income and everything to do with living within your means. That's not a very trendy idea – although I have to say that, as I write, it's a lot trendier than it was a few years ago. We have just experienced one of the great financial crashes in history, and much of it was caused by people being told that they *didn't* have to spend less than they earned – they could borrow their way to financial freedom. I want to write a few words about borrowing money, but first let me introduce you to a little financial magic: it's called compound interest.

It is reputed that Albert Einstein called compound interest the eighth wonder of the world. The best-known illustration of the power of this phenomenon concerns an emperor of China and a chess board. Apparently, the emperor was so excited about the game of chess that he offered the inventor anything he wanted. The inventor replied that he would like one grain of rice for the first square of the chess board, two grains for the second square, four for the third and so on through to the sixty-fourth square. The emperor agreed immediately . . . but had a bit of a rethink when his mathematicians told him that two to the sixty-fourth power is eighteen million trillion. That's a lot of rice; in fact, it's more than enough to cover the entire surface of the earth.

Let me go into the magic of how this works. Imagine your bank pays you interest of 5 per cent and you put £100 in your account. If the bank works out the interest annually, then at the end of the first year you will have £105. If you leave that in for a further year the bank will pay you interest again on your £100 plus interest on the £5 interest you earned in the first year. So at the end of the second year you will have £110.25. If you are a saver, compound interest is brilliant for you. As you sleep, your money is growing. One of the big mistakes I made when I was in my twenties was ignoring the advice of an elderly man who told me to start saving and putting money into a pension plan. Now your grandmother and I didn't earn much money then, but even so I could have put *something* aside.

So is compound interest our friend? Well, not always.

In fact, if we are borrowing money it is our worst enemy because we can get charged interest on the interest. If you really want to see compound interest come into its own, then payday loans are a good example. Now, of course, as their name implies, they are meant to be short-term loans – amounts that are repaid from the borrower's next pay packet. But in reality many people do not repay them on time and the loan is 'rolled over'. The lender says, 'Don't worry about paying us back now – keep the cash, we'll just add it on to the original loan.' And this is where compound interest kicks in. Martin Lewis, the finance expert, heard from one man who wrote: 'My eighteen-year-old daughter borrowed £76 from a payday lender. She now owes £900.'

Lewis illustrates what would happen if you borrowed £200 at an APR of 4214 per cent – a not unusual payday loan APR (they are typically from 1000 to 6000 per cent).[*] If you continually rolled over the loan, after one year you would owe £4,200, after two years, £180,000, and after seven years, £23.5 trillion – more than the entire US national debt (just under £10 trillion).[†]

When it comes to borrowing, the chess board of

---

[*] http://www.bbc.co.uk/consumer/24746198 [accessed 29 April 2014].
[†] http://blog.moneysavingexpert.com/2011/09/21/fact-borrowing-100-at-wongas-apr-costs-more-than-the-us-national-debt-over-14-trillion-after-7-years/ [accessed 29 April 2014].

compound interest will slowly kill your finances. In fact, although not so astronomically terrifying as payday loans (or even worse, money borrowed from loan sharks), if you only make the minimum repayment every month on your credit cards then there's no way back to financial security.

Of course, a normal mortgage that you use to help you buy your home is really in a different category. Nevertheless, the principle of compound interest is the same – although nothing like as dramatic or dangerous. Imagine we borrow £179,000 over twenty-five years at 5 per cent interest. Because of compound interest we will repay a whacking £313,925 by the time our mortgage is finished! (Perhaps that's why it's called a 'mortgage' – it comes from a French word meaning 'death pledge'!)

Make sure that if you have a mortgage, you get one that allows you to make overpayments every month so that if you can ever afford it, you can more quickly repay the amount owed. Why? Because then you diminish the power of compound interest to go on affecting the size of your loan.

Let me show you how it works: if you have a mortgage of £100,000 at 6 per cent interest over twenty-five years, the monthly repayment is £652. Over the twenty-five-year term you will repay £195,000. Of course, there may be times in your life when money is so tight that every penny counts, but remember that however small the overpayment, it will make a difference. Imagine, for instance, that you could somehow manage to increase your repayment by £17.31 a week. You will save £21,200 and your mortgage will be repaid five years earlier!

Now you may be in a position where you think that all this is too late for you – you're up to your neck in credit card debt, or are ten years into your mortgage. Don't let that stop you from taking any action! Begin making more than the minimum repayments on those credit cards. And when that debt is gone, transfer what you have been paying on your cards to overpaying on your mortgage.

There's an old African proverb that says, 'The best time to plant a tree is twenty years ago. The second best time is today.' I really like that. Act now!

20

Other worlds to sing in

D O YOU REMEMBER me mentioning Steve Jobs
during one of our fireside chats? A few years before
his death he gave a speech to the graduating class at Stanford
University, during which he made the following comment:
'If you live each day as if it was your last, someday you'll
most certainly be right.'

It seems strange in an age when we can do so many
things which previous generations could not even have
imagined, that the power of the final enemy to visit each
of us after roughly the same time on earth as the psalmist
suggested thousands of years ago – 'three score years and
ten' – is undiminished.

And this old foe seems to have no respect. He calls
uninvited, at all hours, and with no thought for our

position in society. He asks neither beggar nor billionaire for permission to enter. The old poem puts it well:

> *Death lays his icy hand on kings;*
> *Sceptre and crown*
> *Must tumble down,*
> *And in the dust be equal made*
> *With the poor crooked scythe and spade.**

I thought about all this again one day when I discovered that using Google can be dangerous. One minute I was trying to prove the quizmaster wrong and find the name of the first American in space (it was Alan Shepard – the quizmaster was right), the next I'd hit a wrong key and was faced with a page that offered to work out my life expectancy!

Who could resist knowing how long they've got left? Not me. I filled in a zillion boxes. Yes, I do wear seatbelts. No, the person in whose car I am normally a passenger does not regularly get drunk. In the past year I smoked no cigarettes, had only one sexual partner, and was an 'occasional exerciser' (I couldn't bear to tick the box that said 'sedentary' – it made me sound dead already). After that, there were just a few more boxes to complete – my

---

* James Shirley, 'Death the Leveller'.

height, my weight, and a quick tour of my family's medical history. Now I was ready to click on the box that said 'Calculate Now'.

And it's here that I hesitated. Did I really want to know? Would I not rather continue with the illusion that although everybody else dies, somehow *I* will slip through the net and generations to come will say, 'He's good for his age. How old is he?' 'Oh, five hundred and ten!'

Sebastien Chamfort tells the story of a woman of ninety who said to ninety-five-year-old M. de Fontenelle, 'Death has forgotten us.'

M. de Fontenelle put his finger to his lips and said, 'Shh . . .'

But perhaps hitting that 'Calculate Now' button is a good idea. The good book urges us to 'Number our days that we may get a heart of wisdom.'*

I wonder why that is so important? Could it be that if I did 'number my days' then I would let those who offend me off the hook a little more easily? Could it be that actually seeing the number might cause me to telephone that relative I haven't spoken to for ten years since the silly row at the wedding, and finally make up with them? Was it possible that actually gazing at this figure would affect how I dealt with the little things and make me get

* Psalm 90:12 ESV.

less screwed up about a faulty microwave or a lost TV remote control? Could it be that I will stop taking myself so seriously and be a little less proud over my petty successes and a little easier on myself over my apparent disasters? Could it be that as I sense those years slipping by so quickly, I will be more willing to take risks with people, or even with myself? Could it be that I will make sure that every day I tell those who matter to me that I love them? Could it be . . .?

I remember thinking to myself that if only half of that was true, then it was worth knowing. I closed my eyes and hit the 'Calculate Now' box. Then I opened my eyes one at a time. In an instant the computer had worked out for me what the ancient poet urged me to ponder in my heart. The figure that sat in the box seemed to gaze at me with neither congratulation nor sympathy. I sighed. So many years left . . .

. . . and so few.

But even if I believed the date patiently flashing at me that day on my computer screen, that knowledge doesn't answer the *really* big question. No, for that I must look not to my calculator, but to my calendar. The one I use is made up of boxes, and each has a date written above it. Every day I am pulled from one box into another. And each box has no patience with the one before it. At one second past midnight, I am pulled through a door into the next box – and for the next twenty-four hours my life will be played out within its walls.

If I am foolish, or simply too preoccupied to reflect, I can believe that there is an endless supply of boxes waiting for me. But there is not. And for that reason I must try to live my life in the *present* box, grasping the preciousness of *this* moment. And this is vital, for although we may find it hard to grasp our own mortality, Steve Jobs was right: there *is* a last box. And this one has no doors that can lead me into the next day.

The biggest question in the universe is this: does that last box have no doors because it is just a coffin and death is the end? Or does it have no doors because death is a beginning and that particular box, unlike all the others . . .

. . . *has no walls?*

What do you think?

Here's a story that I've told to people all across the world. It's about a boy whose parents owned one of the first telephones. They lived on the plains in America, and the wooden box with a handle was installed in their farmhouse kitchen. The boy thought it a wonderful machine. His mother would wind it up and say, 'Information please,' and a lady would reply, 'This is Information.' He said, 'It was incredible. Information Please would get you a number, tell you the time and even the weather.'

One day when he was in the house alone, he banged

his thumb with a hammer. He said, 'There was no point crying because there was nobody in. And then I remembered the telephone. I got a stool, stood on it, and reached up to the handset. "Information Please," I said between sobs.

'The lady replied in her standard way, "This is Information. How can I help you?"

'"I've banged my thumb with a hammer," I said.

'"Is your mummy in?" Information Please asked.

'"No."

'"Is your daddy in?"

'"No."

'"Is it bleeding?"

'I turned my thumb over and checked it out. "No."

'Information Please said, "Can you get to the ice box?"

'"Yes."

'"Hold some ice against it."

'It worked! After that I rang Information Please for *anything*. Information Please helped me with my geography homework: she told me where Philadelphia was. Information Please taught me to spell *disappear*. And when my pet canary died and I cried down the phone and said, "Why would God make something that can sing so beautifully and let it die?" Information Please said, "Paul, you must always remember there are other worlds to sing in."

'And then, when I was nine, my parents moved to Boston. I missed my mentor terribly. Information Please belonged in that old wooden box back at home and I didn't believe that she could live in the new plastic phone we had now. Yet, as I grew into my teens, the memories of those childhood conversations never left me. Often in moments of doubt or confusion I would recall the wonderful sense of security I had when I knew that I could call Information Please and get the right answer. I appreciated now how very patient, understanding and kind she was to have spent time on a little boy. I never rang her again . . . until I was twenty-four years old.

'I was making a trip one day and my plane put down in an airport near where we used to live. I had about half an hour to wait and was sitting in the airport lounge when I saw a telephone. I thought, "I wonder . . ." I dialled my old hometown operator and said, "Information please" . . . Miraculously I heard again the voice I knew so well, "This is Information."

'I asked, "Could you teach me to spell *disappear*?"

'There was a long pause and then she replied, "I expect that thumb is better by now!"

'I said, "Have you any idea what you meant to me?"

'She said, "Have you any idea what you meant to *me*? We never had children and I used to look forward to your calls. Silly, wasn't it?" It didn't seem silly to me, but I didn't say so. I asked her if I could call her again when I came back to the area. "Please do," she said. "Just ask for Sally."

'After that, I rang Sally whenever I was in the area and we would talk. One day, though, I dialled the number and a different voice answered, "This is Information."

'I asked for Sally. "Are you a friend?" the woman said.

'"Yes," I replied, "an old friend."

'There was a pause and the operator said, "I'm so sorry to have to tell you that Sally died five weeks ago."

'Before I could thank her and hang up, she said, "Wait a minute. Did you say your name was Villard?"

'"Yes."

'"Well, Sally left a message for you. She said that if you happen to ring we must be sure to give it to you: *Paul, you must always remember there are other worlds to sing in.*"'

21

Be my best friend

ICAN'T REMEMBER WHERE I left my glasses, but I remember an occasion over half a century ago in my school playground in the minutest detail. Every school playground is a place of wonderful joy and incredible tragedy. It's as if we practise there the attitudes, the encouragements and the cruelty that one day we will unleash on the wider world. And my junior school play-ground was no exception. I was ten years old and it was a Monday morning when I decided to approach the most popular boy in the class. In many ways, he was my hero. While other boys dreamed of being the Lone Ranger or Robin Hood, my daily prayer was much nearer home: 'Dear God, make me like Roger Lewis.'

Roger was tall, good-looking and clever. It was Roger

everybody wanted on their team. Not for Roger the igno-
miny of being left to last when teams were picked and
hearing the captains say to each other, 'You have him!'
'No, you have him!' It was Roger the girls wanted to kiss
behind the toilets, Roger who always broke the tape first,
and Roger who came top in the tests. In some ways it
seemed so unfair. It was as if, just before his birth, heaven
had found a box full of talent, good looks and lucky
breaks, and decided to use them all up on Roger – only
to discover a week later that they were actually meant to
be shared out among our whole class. But by then it was
too late: Roger had got the lot.

As I watched him from across the playground my heart
was pounding. He stood holding court and, as ever, surrounded by admirers. I agonised as to whether to go
through with my plan. Finally, taking a deep breath, I
walked across to him. His groupies looked surprised to
see me, but even they sensed that something significant
was about to happen and parted to let me through. I felt
myself redden and then suddenly blurted out the question
I had been practising in front of a mirror – and, on one
occasion, in front of my mother – all the previous
weekend: 'Roger, do you want to be my best friend?' I had
considered offering Roger a reciprocal arrangement
whereby I would be his number one too, but I had bottled
out at the last moment. This was easier; he didn't have to

pick me, just allow me to have *him* as my best friend. What did he have to lose?

I don't think he heard me at first, and I repeated my question – although quieter than last time. 'Do you want to be my best friend?'

This time Roger heard, but I soon wished he hadn't because he started to laugh, and then those around him joined in until they were all holding their sides. I had a nickname at school and soon a cry was echoing around the playground of Roath Park Juniors: 'Who'd want Parsnips as a best friend! Who'd want Parsnips as a best friend?'

Thankfully, a bit later on in life, somebody did. But the road to close friendships is, at least for some, not an easy one. We live in a society where we often find it hard, especially if we are men, to forge deep relationships. And yet the studies show time and again that friendships could be the best predictor of our daily happiness and satisfaction with life. In 2004, researchers at Duke University Medical Centre explored the protective effect of friendships.* They found that having three or more friends helped people live significantly longer.

---

* B. H. Brummett et al., 'Characteristics of Socially Isolated Patients with Coronary Artery Disease who are at Elevated Risk for Mortality', *Psychosomatic Medicine* 63, 2001, pp. 267–272.

But it's not just about longevity: friendships have long been proven to improve our health and life satisfaction. It seems we do not need a wide breadth of friends, but we do need *quality* friendships.[*] Each person needs a few very deep friendships in order to thrive. Lonely people suffer psychologically and physically. Eugene Kennedy, a professor of psychology at Loyola University, Chicago, said, 'Friendship has a profound effect on your physical well-being. Having good relationships improves health and lifts depressions. You don't necessarily need drugs or medical treatment to accomplish this, just friends.'[†]

I have to tell you, I have been blessed over the years with incredible friends, but I don't think I am a natural in this area. I have, however, observed some people who I believe are masters at making and keeping close friends. Allow me to share just one of the lessons I have learned from them. I confess that it can be very difficult to put into practice – in fact, some of us never manage to negotiate this first hurdle of building deep friendships: vulnerability.

Many people have never had one minute in their whole

---

[*] Considering Gallup 2005 alongside Brummet et al., 2001; also H. Cheng and A. Furnham, 'Personality, peer relations, and self-confidence as predictors of happiness and loneliness', *Journal of Adolescence* 25 (3), 2002, pp. 327–339.

[†] Eugene Kennedy, 'The Friendship Factor', *Prevention*, 2002.

lifetime where they could let their defences down and
share their deepest feelings with another person. Often,
people will say to a psychiatrist or psychotherapist, 'You
are the first person I have ever been completely honest
with.' One psychotherapist said, 'I sometimes wonder
whether the reluctance to be known by a friend or a
spouse leads to the need to see me.'

But to make ourselves vulnerable is not easy. Most of
us vacillate between the impulse to share ourselves with
others and the urge to protect ourselves; we long to be
known and to remain hidden – the temptation to wear
masks is very strong. And we are afraid of rejection – we
believe that if people really knew us they would not like
us, let alone love us. Yet self-disclosure actually has the
opposite effect: when we reveal ourselves to people, they
are drawn to us. Honesty produces friendship; we like
people to disclose something of themselves to us, and as
we reveal ourselves to others, so they feel more able to let
us into their lives.

Practising vulnerability may mean saying to a friend in
the student union one night, 'I'm not really coping with
this course. I feel totally out of my depth.' It could mean
saying to a work colleague, 'I know we're all saying we'll
find good jobs after the redundancy, but I'm not sure I
will. It's keeping me awake at nights thinking about it.' It
may be offering a cup of coffee to a colleague at work

whose child has got into trouble with the police and saying, 'We had some trouble with one of our kids a few years ago . . .'

Friendships help make us strong, but the irony is that a little *weakness* helps them grow. People who make deep and lasting friendships may be young or old, introverts or extroverts, but they have got used to taking the masks off – they allow others to see into their hearts.

One of the books I love reading to you grandchildren is *The Velveteen Rabbit*.* I think it sums up so much about friendship and vulnerability. Here's a short extract:

'What is REAL?' asked the Rabbit one day, when they were lying side by side near the nursery fender, before Nana came to tidy the room. 'Does it mean having things that buzz inside you and a stick-out handle?'

'Real isn't how you are made,' said the Skin Horse. 'It's a thing that happens to you. When a child loves you for a long, long time, not just to play with, but REALLY loves you, then you become Real.'

'Does it hurt?' asked the Rabbit.

'Sometimes,' said the Skin Horse, for he was

* Margery Williams, *The Velveteen Rabbit* (first published 1922).

always truthful. 'When you are Real you don't mind being hurt.'

'Does it happen all at once, like being wound up,' he asked, 'or bit by bit?'

'It doesn't happen all at once,' said the Skin Horse. 'You become. It takes a long time. That's why it doesn't happen often to people who break easily, or have sharp edges, or who have to be carefully kept. Generally, by the time you are Real, most of your hair has been loved off, and your eyes drop out and you get loose in the joints and very shabby. But these things don't matter at all, because once you are Real you can't be ugly, except to people who don't understand.'

You can't wear your heart on your sleeve with everybody and sometimes it's not easy to find those whom we feel we can trust, but we *must* find those people. If you want acquaintances, tell them your successes.

If you want friends, tell them your fears.

22
Thieves of joy

WHEN YOUR GRANDMOTHER and I were teenagers in the 1960s, we loved the music that was around then – and we still do. Not so long ago we went to a 'Sounds of the Sixties' concert. Just looking at the publicity filled me with anticipation. For two hours I was going to be breathing the same air as some of the greatest names from my teenage years: The Searchers, Freddy and the Dreamers, Manfred Mann and a host of others.

My first decent kiss was to the sound of 'Do wha diddy diddy dum diddy do' and I remember putting on ice-blue jeans and a leather jacket to sneak into the Kennard dance hall and hear local groups try to play 'Ferry Cross the Mersey'. Forty years later, as I walked into St David's Hall in Cardiff on that rainy Tuesday evening, I felt as if I was about to step straight back into those wonder years. Happy days, here I come!

The first shock was the audience. They were so *old*. What were all these ancient people doing at a pop concert to hear my groups? At least, they were old from the neck up. Below that they looked as if they were sixteen: leather bomber jackets, gold chains, winklepicker shoes and pink socks. If I kept my eyes low, I could believe I was still in the Kennard; lift them, and concerns about how to keep false teeth from slipping out flooded my mind.

The next shock was the groups themselves. They looked older than the audience. The lead singer of the Swinging Blue Jeans apologised that he couldn't leap about because he'd hurt his back. No amount of make-up, toupees and, on one ancient rocker, brown head paint, could hide the dreadful fact that time had touched my heroes too. The music was still great, but as I walked back through the rain to the car park I was in a sober mood. And it was then that an even deeper shock hit me – the realisation that those teenage days weren't as great as I'd been remembering them. Girlfriends finished with me, maths teachers scared me, best friends hurt me, and pimples attacked my face like barbarian hordes descending on the Romans. The ancient book of Ecclesiastes – the name of which refers to its writer, 'the philosopher' – has a fascinating warning in it: 'Don't ask, "Why were the old days better than these?" It is not wise to ask such questions.'

There are two thieves of joy, and they are sister and brother. The first is the one warned against in the old wisdom book: a rose-tinted yearning that the past might return – better summers, snowier winters, trains that run on time, family Christmases without conflict. We sigh as we tell people how great life used to be.

Its sibling turns our eyes not back, but forward. A friend of mine who is a clinical psychologist told me that most people believe a future event will make them happy – when I win the lottery, move house, or pass my exams. This can include even quite small events – when I get that new gadget or see my friends on Saturday night. But then he said, really happy people manage to grasp a little happiness *now*: because now is all we've really got. Somebody put it like this: 'Yesterday is history. Tomorrow is a mystery. Today is a gift – that's why we call it the *present*.'

As you know, the point of inviting you into my study for these little chats has been all about sharing the lessons learned by older people (including me!) down through the years. Just listen in to this conversation that a young woman of twenty-five had with one particular elderly lady, Martha, a nursing home resident aged eighty-seven.

'Oh, Martha, I seem to have made such a mess of my life. All I ever wanted to do is to be happy.'

'Join the club then, dear. The whole world wants to be happy. But the problem for most people is that they are *pursuing* happiness – trying to catch it.'

'What do you mean?'

'I mean that for most people happiness is something they believe they will have when something happens in the future.'

'What's wrong with that?'

'Well, happiness can run faster than you . . .'

Claire remembers putting her hand over Martha's and moving her finger across the brown spots and the bulging veins, 'Explain please.'

'When you try to catch happiness it always moves away from you,' Martha answered, patting Claire's hand with her own. 'Have you ever tried to catch a butterfly?'

'Yes, when I was young I used to chase them around my garden trying to catch them.'

'And did you ever catch one while it was flying?'

'I don't think so, but I do remember catching one that had stopped on a ledge. I swooped and covered it with my hand.'

'And that, my dear,' Martha had chuckled with

delight, 'is how you catch happiness. You must not pursue it – you must surprise it.'

'I don't understand.'

'Really happy people have found that the secret of happiness is not to run after it, but to catch it when it least expects you to find it – and that is always *now.* You must learn to capture the moment. Of course, I'm not really talking about the very terrible things that happen to people, but so often in life generally, happiness is not so much concerned with circumstances, but with the way we treat them. Look at us, holding hands together. Do you feel happy now?'

'Oh, Martha, I can't say I feel happy – my life's a bit of a mess at the moment – but I can tell you this: just now, in this room, I feel at peace and there is no place I would rather be than here with you.'

'There – you've caught it. Just when happiness wasn't looking, you swooped! I do declare, you are one of the cleverest young women I have ever met.'

If the two thieves of joy are a hankering after a perfect past on the one hand, and a yearning for a change of some kind in the future, then what is it that they steal from us? The truth is so terrifying we can hardly face it: they steal our only opportunity in life to find fulfilment, happiness and peace.

They steal *today.*

23

Thirty-fourth!

I WONDER IF YOU will like going to school? I didn't understand secondary school at all. Let me try to explain what I mean by that. In those days, eleven-year-olds had to take an examination called the 11 Plus, to decide what type of school they went on to. Children who failed it went to what were called secondary modern schools, which had an emphasis on practical skills. Those who passed the exam went to grammar schools, which concentrated on academic subjects. I remember my mother running upstairs to my bedroom and telling me I had passed. I was the only kid in my street ever to have done it.

It was George Bernard Shaw who wrote, 'There are two great tragedies in life. One is not to get your heart's desire. The other is to get it.' I had got the desire of my heart, but the second I started grammar school, wearing the brand-new uniform that my mother had been able to buy by cleaning other people's houses, I knew it had not been a good idea. The kids at this school were different from me. They spoke differently. Their houses were different – they had inside toilets, bathrooms and toilet paper. (Don't ask – even now I can't look at an old copy of the *South Wales Echo* without a hundred memories flooding back!) But most different of all, either they or their parents seemed to understand how to study effectively. We had only three books in our home: an atlas, a Bible and *The Shorter Oxford Dictionary*. Other kids' parents could afford tutors; I had never *heard* of a tutor.

I did badly at school. My report for the Easter term of 1963 records the fact that out of the thirty-four kids in my class I had come thirty-fourth. In those days, the teachers used to read out the class order beginning with who was in top place. I'm sure you can imagine that if you hadn't heard your name by the time the teacher got to the late teens, you started to panic. Into the early twenties . . . the late twenties . . . still nothing. By the time we were into the thirties, I was planning to faint. And, finally, we were down to the last two names: it was just me and Arthur Harries. I looked across the classroom at Arthur and Arthur looked at me. The silence in the room was palpable. The teacher hesitated – playing with us. He was Nero and the class was the crowd in the Colosseum. Somebody was going to die. And then, as if whispered from another planet, I heard Arthur's name.

On that day I wouldn't have minded never seeing any of my classmates ever again, let alone have contemplated attending a school reunion. Anyway it is said that only people who believe they have been successful are likely to attend such affairs. There is a story about a boy called Charlie who was hopeless at everything in school. He came last in every test and every race. In fact he was called Waster Charlie. On the night of the school reunion there were BMWs, Mercedes and the occasional Porsche in the car park as accountants, hospital consultants and other luminaries gathered to tell each other what a great job they had made of life. One business consultant remarked that they were unlikely to see Waster Charlie!

Almost as he said it, a brand-new Bentley purred up to the front door. A chauffeur got out, opened the rear door, and out stepped a tanned and immaculately dressed Charlie.

As he came through the door there was silence in the room, but eventually somebody had the courage to ask the question that was on everybody's lips. 'Charlie, how on earth did you do it?'

Charlie seemed happy to tell his story. 'Well,' he said, 'after I left school I couldn't get a job. And then one day my mate asked me to help him build a shed in his garden. It was easy and I thought I could do it. The next day, I went round to the builders' yard and asked if they had any old bits of wood they didn't want. They must have felt sorry for me because they gave me some off-cuts. I made my first shed and sold it for a fiver. With the money, I bought some more wood, and this time I built two sheds and sold them. And that's how I went on. By the end of a year, I had made and sold seventeen sheds. And then I got a letter saying that a distant auntie from Australia had died and left me ten million quid. And I thought: *stuff making sheds!*'

It's probably best not to rely on the legacy thing for success in life! But to be serious, I truly believe that *no one* should be written off as a failure in life when there is still time to change – and certainly not when they are still at school. I have written elsewhere of the men and women who helped me get from being at the bottom of the class to experiencing the incredible opportunities that I have today. Suffice to say, I believe that, with kids, it's best not to read their school reports as though they are a prophecy of their future lives. In other words, don't read the score at half time. Some of us develop a little later, and when we find something that lights our fire, everything changes. And what you can achieve when somebody you respect believes in you – a mother, father, sports coach, boss or teacher – is simply life-changing.

In an old box in my study is my school report book. It has bound into it every report I received from age eleven to eighteen. As I have already intimated, it doesn't make pretty reading. Most pages are filled with comments like 'weak', 'fairly weak', 'poor' and, on one page, 'he has been issued with text books and has attended some lessons'. One of the comments at first said 'very good', but 'good' has been deleted in pen and the word 'satisfactory' put in its place. What on earth does 'very satisfactory' mean, for goodness' sake? On one report when I was fourteen my form teacher has written: 'A disgraceful result. He is making no use of what little ability he has.'

I did poorly in academic terms in that school, as I have said, but people came into my life who believed in me – who convinced me that what my form teacher had written about 'little ability' was not necessarily true. And even if it was true, they persuaded me that you can achieve more with little ability if you use it, than with a lot of ability if you don't. Those people changed my life. Within twelve years I was a partner in a legal practice and lecturing to thousands of lawyers every year through the legal consultancy that I had helped to found.

The truth is that my form teacher had every right to say whether or not I had passed examinations, was absent from school, or was disruptive in class. But what he did not have the right to do was to dismiss my 'little ability'. This is for the simple reason that 'ability' in a fourteen-year-old boy can as easily be a seed as a full-grown tree. I remember reading that comment. It was as if he had put me in a box with 'Losers' marked on it. But although school reports are important, there are many things they don't measure. They don't measure emotional intelligence; they don't measure the ability some kids have to network or do deals; they often don't allow for the fact that some children develop a little later in life; and they certainly don't allow for the fact that when we find something that captures our hearts and our imaginations, it changes everything.

As I looked through that report book again the other day, it occurred to me that the really important page is still blank. For some reason, my school didn't fill it in. But actually, the wonderful truth is that this page is still blank in all our report books, no matter what age we are. This report will be written at the end of our lives, and it is not necessarily determined by past performances or even failures. I have reproduced it on the next page. You will notice that A. Sinclair, MA, MEd, has his name at the bottom, but the good news for me is that although he may have thought otherwise, he will not be the one filling it in . . .

notice that A. Sinclair, M.A., M.Ed. has his name at the

Final Report

Signed

A. SINCLAIR, M.A., M.Ed.

....
Head Master

Date.................................19.........

24

The long walk home

I WONDER IF THERE may come a time in your life when you feel you've really blown it and there's no way back. Of course, I have no idea whether you have any religious beliefs at all, but whether you do or don't, I'd like you to consider for a moment a story that Jesus told.* It has become one of the best-known pieces of prose in the world. In fact, when I was studying English Literature, my lecturer (who told us quite clearly that she was 'not religious at all') said that she thought this little parable was perhaps the greatest short story ever written.

It is about a father who had two children. Now if you ever become a parent and have more than one child, you

---

* Luke 15:11–32.

may well find that your offspring have entirely different personalities and characteristics. Often you will find that one will be perfectly behaved and the other will test you on a daily basis. The two boys in this story are like that. It is often called the 'Parable of the Prodigal Son', but actually it is a story about both children: one compliant and well behaved, the other a hell-raiser. The second brother asks for his share of his father's estate and leaves home as fast as he can. While he is partying, his older brother works diligently in the father's business. But then the younger brother falls on hard times – he ends up penniless and friendless. And at the moment when he is at his lowest, he thinks again of home and decides to start the long walk back.

Of course he has no idea how his father, whose heart he has broken, will receive him, so he prepares a speech which, in essence, asks if he can work for bed and breakfast until he gets on his feet. What he doesn't know is that every day since he left, his father has been looking down the road to see if he's coming home.

Some years ago, a woman wrote to me and said that when her daughter was eighteen she had walked out of their home after a row. She didn't get in touch, and they didn't know whether she was alive or dead. At night, as this mother and her husband turned off the lights before they went to bed, she would always say to him, 'Leave the porch light on.' And every Christmas she would put a little Christmas tree in the front of the house, its lights shining, just as she used to when her daughter was a child.

That couple didn't see their daughter for six years. Then one day, out of the blue, she knocked on their door and fell into her mother's arms. She said:

> Mum, I so often wanted to come home, but I was too ashamed. But sometimes, in the early hours of the morning, I would drive my car into our street and just sit there. I used to gaze at the houses and every one of them was dark apart from our house: you always left a light on. And at Christmas I would do the same: just sit there in the darkness and look at the Christmas tree you had put outside – I knew it was for me.

The parent in the old story is not so different from that mother. When the 'prodigal' son is way down the road, the father sees him and starts running towards him. The son tries to get his speech out, but the old boy just won't let him – he is hugging him so hard he can hardly breathe.

And then the older brother comes on the scene. He is judgemental, bitter, and with no shortage of vitriol for the father: 'Why are we throwing a party for *him*? He has wasted your money and his life.' What he doesn't know is that his father can't help himself; he loves his son so much that the past doesn't matter right now. All that matters is that his boy is home.

Of course, the father in the story really symbolises God and his willingness to forgive us and welcome us back. And because of that, I want you to know that whatever you do, you can always come home. If your mum and dad are alive I'm sure they'll run down that road towards you, and certainly if I'm still about I'll whiz towards you on my Zimmer frame. But even if, for any reason, we are not there – another father will be waiting.

And there will be a light on.

25

Anyway

M Y DEAR HARRY, Lily, Evie, Jackson and Freddie
. . . and any other grandchildren who may yet
come!

I can't believe that our talks together have come to an
end so quickly – let's do it again soon! I have loved sharing
with you some of the life lessons I've learned – some of
them the *very* hard way and many from people far wiser
than me. As I thought about our final session together, I
wondered what the last offering from the Wisdom House
could be. That little problem was solved for me less than
an hour ago when somebody read to me some words that
used to hang on the wall in Mother Teresa's office.

Try to remember them:

People are often unreasonable, irrational, and self-centred. Forgive them anyway.

If you are kind, people may accuse you of selfish, ulterior motives. Be kind anyway.

If you are successful, you will win some unfaithful friends and some genuine enemies. Succeed anyway.

If you are honest and sincere, people may deceive you. Be honest and sincere anyway.

What you spend years creating, others could destroy overnight. Create anyway.

If you find serenity and happiness, some may be jealous. Be happy anyway.

The good you do today will often be forgotten. Do good anyway.

Give the best you have, and it will never be enough. Give your best anyway.

In the final analysis, it is between you and God. It was never between you and them *anyway*.

Thanks for those times we've sat together in the chairs in front of my fireplace. I know you were only there in my imagination but, only a few days ago, you were all at our house for real: Lily was fussing around cooking lunch for everybody on her plastic toy stove, Evie was causing mayhem, Jackson and Freddie were sitting there smiling and looking as if they couldn't wait to get into what Evie was doing, and Harry was strumming his pretend guitar and singing 'The Gambler' – a song I must confess that I taught him myself.

As I have pictured sharing the lessons of *The Wisdom House* with you as grown men and women, I have wondered what the future holds for each of you. There are so many prayers I could say for you, but let me end by making a prayer of something written by Jonathan Swift – I noticed a copy of his book *Gulliver's Travels* on one of your bookshelves the other day:

'May you live all the days of your life.'